Spanish Word Puzzles

Frank Nuessel, Ph.D.

Department of Classical and Modern Languages

University of Louisville

Louisville, Kentucky

BARRON'S

For Marcel Danesi

All inquiries should be addressed to:
Barron's Educational Series, Inc.
250 Wireless Boulevard
Hauppauge, New York 11788
http://www.barronseduc.com

ISBN-13: 978-0-7641-3303-9
ISBN-10: 0-7641-3303-9

Printed in the United States of America
9 8 7 6 5 4 3 2 1

Spanish Word Puzzles

Contents

Preface

Everybody loves to solve a crossword puzzle! If you're a busy person, with little time to spend on long and complicated Spanish-language textbooks, but still able to find a minute to solve crosswords and other kinds of puzzles, this is the book for you. *Spanish Word Puzzles* is designed to help you learn the basics of Spanish in an enjoyable, stimulating, and effortless way. All you need is a love for solving word puzzles!

The book is intended for English-speaking students of Spanish. It will help you expand your vocabulary, reinforce your knowledge of grammar, and entertain you at the same time! The puzzles cover common topics such as food, clothing, plants, verbs, and Hispanic culture. They come in a variety of formats (crosswords, scrambled letters, cryptograms, and word searches) and in increasing levels of difficulty—from easy to challenging.

Learners at different stages of linguistic knowledge will find a variety of puzzles within their abilities, given the large selection provided here—100 in total! The best thing to do, however, is to start with the easiest and work your way right through to the most challenging ones. At the end of the book, you have the answers to all puzzles and a handy word finder that lists all the words and expressions you will need to solve the 100 puzzles. Although the puzzles get harder as you progress, the language does not! This book is intended for beginning and intermediate English-speaking learners of Spanish.

Spanish Word Puzzles will bring you hours and hours of learning fun. All you need is a pencil and a knack for solving puzzles!

Easy Puzzles

The puzzles in this section are classified as easy because the types of clues you are given to solve them are of the simple variety, such as English equivalents, and so on. Also, you will be given plenty of hints, more so than in any of the remaining sections. Have fun!

CRUCIGRAMAS (CROSSWORDS)
En casa (At Home)

1. Las habitaciones y sus partes (Rooms and Their Parts)

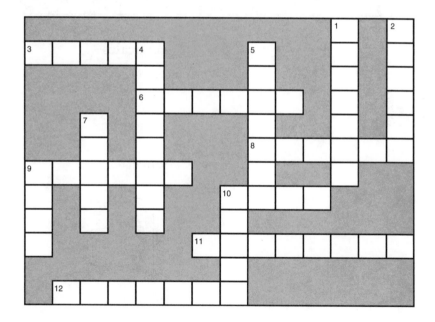

Horizontales	Verticales
3. Wall	1. Dining room
6. Basement	2. Door
8. Bedroom	4. Pantry
9. Kitchen	5. Window
10. Living room	7. Ceiling
11. Study	9. House
12. Closet	10. Floor

2. En la mesa (At the table)

Horizontales

5.

6.

7. Pepper shaker

12.

13. Napkin

15.

Verticales

1.

2. Saucer

3.

4. Wineglass

8. Knife

9.

10. Fork

11. Tablecloth

14.

3. Los muebles (Furniture)

Horizontales

2. Drawer

4. Piece of furniture

6.

10. Writing desk

12.

13.

14. Mirror

Verticales

1. Chest of drawers

3.

5. Stool

7. Table

8.

9.

11. Dresser

4. Objetos caseros (Household Objects)

Horizontales

2.

3. Stove

7.

8.

Verticales

1.

4. Telephone

5.

6. Doorbell

9. Light

5. El ocio y los pasatiempos (Leisure Time and Pastimes)

Horizontales

3.

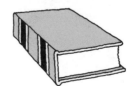

6.

7. Soap opera

10. Cable

11.

Verticales

1. Crossword puzzle

2.

4. Web

5.

8.

9. Game

La familia y la gente (Family and People)

6. La familia (Family)

Horizontales	Verticales
1. Son	1. Daughter
5. Mother-in-law	2. Aunt
6. Sister-in-law	3. Brother-in-law
9. Grandmother	4. Father-in-law
10. Grandson	7. Grandfather
11. Uncle	8. Father
12. Mother	10. Granddaughter

7. **La gente** (People)

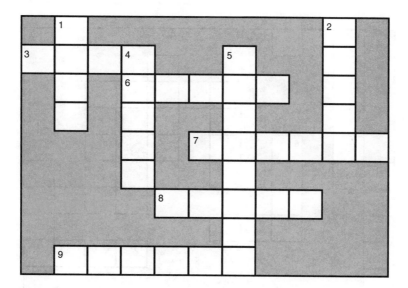

Horizontales

3. Child (female)

6. Woman

7. Man

8. Friend (male)

9. Mrs.

Verticales

1. Child (male)

2. Mister

4. Friend (female)

5. Miss

8. El cuerpo (The Body)

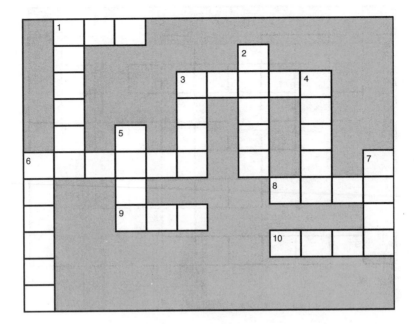

Horizontales

1.

3.

6.

8. Face

9.

10. Finger

Verticales

1.

2. Lip
3.

4.

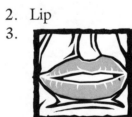

5. Hair

6. Neck

7.

9. La constitución física (Physique)

Horizontales

4. Slender
6.
8. Beautiful
9.

Verticales

1.
2. Red-haired
3. Brunette
5.
7. Ugly

10. La personalidad (Personality)

Horizontales
3. Liberal
4. Shy
8. Conservative
9. Serious
10. Reserved
11. Adventurous

Verticales
1. Funny
2. Withdrawn
5. Gregarious
6. Sad
7. Happy

LETRAS REVUELTAS (SCRAMBLED LETTERS)

Las nociones básicas (Basic Notions)

In the first column are scrambled letters of the word or expression to which the clue in the middle applies. Write the answer in the third column by unscrambling the letters.

11. Los números (Numbers)

Scrambled Letters	Clues	Answers
ceno	11	__ __ __ __
eeintv	20	__ __ __ __ __ __
nice	100	__ __ __ __
ientrta	30	__ __ __ __ __ __ __
lim	1,000	__ __ __
testnae	70	__ __ __ __ __ __ __
ceaortc	14	__ __ __ __ __ __ __
eites	7	__ __ __ __ __
nicesodtos	200	__ __ __ __ __ __ __ __ __ __
antenvo	90	__ __ __ __ __ __ __

12. La hora (Telling Time)

Scrambled Letters	Clues	Answers
eiaoemnchd	12:00 (A.M.)	__ __ __ __ __ __ __ __ __ __
eioíamdd	12:00 (P.M.)	__ __ __ __ __ __ __
onche	opposite of day	__ __ __ __ __
aíd	opposite of night	__ __ __
asl sod y iaemd	two thirty	__ __ __ __ __ __ __
		__ __ __ __ __
sla eeuvn	nine o'clock	__ __ __ __ __ __ __ __
drtea	afternoon	__ __ __ __ __
sal choo y rtcauo	8:15	__ __ __ __ __ __ __ __
		__ __ __ __ __
al nua ne uoptn	1 o'clock sharp	__ __ __ __ __ __ __
		__ __ __ __
ñnmaaa	opposite of evening	__ __ __ __ __ __

13. El tiempo (Weather)

Scrambled Letters	*Clues*	*Answers*
áest baludno	It's cloudy.	— — — —
		— — — — — — —
chea íorf	It's cold.	— — — — — — — —
aehc tnvoie	It's windy.	— — —
		— — — — — —
heac oalcr	It's hot.	— — — — — — — — —
eivna	It's snowing.	— — — — —
eeuvll	It's raining.	— — — — — —
tseá eeaoddspj	It's clear.	— — — —
		— — — — — — — —
stáe úeomdh	It's humid.	— — — —
		— — — — — —
euartn	It's thundering.	— — — — — —
chea oefsrc	It's cool.	— — — —
		— — — — — —

14. Los colores (Colors)

Scrambled Letters	Clues	Answers
oojr	red	— — — —
luza	blue	— — — —
eedrv	green	— — — — —
rrmnóa	brown	— — — — — —
ooadrm	purple	— — — — — —
aonlbc	white	— — — — — —
egron	black	— — — — —
aaaaonnjdr	orange	— — — — — — — — — —
llmraaoi	yellow	— — — — — — — —
ooadsr	pink	— — — — — —

15. Términos opuestos (Opposites)

Scrambled Letters	Clues	Answers
eulcd	sweet	— — — — —
oaargm	bitter	— — — — — —
ddrnooe	round	— — — — — — —
uaaoddrc	square	— — — — — — — —
eauvs	soft	— — — — —
rodu	hard	— — — —
smptciiáo	nice	— — — — — — — — —
áaiionpttc	unpleasant	— — — — — — — — — —
grola	long	— — — — —
ootrc	short	— — — — —

CRUCIGRAMAS (CROSSWORDS)

La ropa y el calzado (Clothing and Footwear)

16. La ropa (Clothing)

Horizontales

3. Jacket

5.

8. Socks

9.

10. Stockings

11.

Verticales

1.

2. Pants

4.

6. T-shirt

7.

17. Otra ropa (Other Clothing)

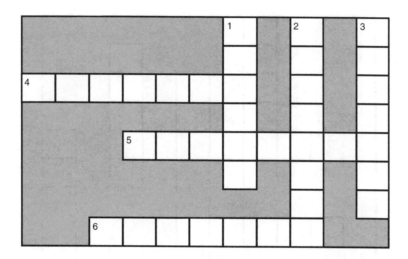

Horizontales

4.

5. Belt

6.

Verticales

1.

2. Hat

3.

18. Las joyas (Jewelry)

Horizontales

5.

6. Necklace

7.

Verticales

1. Chain

2.

3. Bracelet

4.

19. El calzado (Footwear)

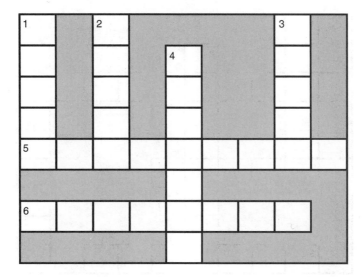

Horizontales

5.

6. Shoelaces

Verticales

1.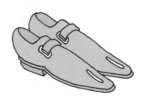

2. Heel

3. Sole

4.

20. Vestirse o no (Getting Dressed or Not)

Horizontales

4. To undress

5. To try on

6. To put on

Verticales

1. To wear

2. To take off

3. To get dressed

CRIPTOGRAMAS (CRYPTOGRAMS)
Los saludos y la conversación básica
(Greetings and Basic Conversation)

In this section, a specific number will correspond to a specific letter of the alphabet in all the cryptograms. For example, if you establish that 1 = A, 8 = D, and 21 = T in any of the five puzzles, then you can go ahead and substitute that letter for each occurrence of the digit in the remaining puzzles. To help you start, you are given a few substitutions. Clue: Determine the numbers for the vowels first and then determine the numbers for the consonants. Good luck!

21. Los saludos (Greetings)

Hello! ¡__ __ __ A!
        11 4 13 1

Good-bye! ¡__ D __ ´__!
           1 8 3 4 20

22. Más saludos (More Greetings)

How are you? ¿__ ´__ __ __   __ __ T ´__?
              7 4 14 4   2 20 21 1 20

Very well. __ __ __   __ __ __ __
            14 5 24   6 3 2 15

23. La presentación (Introduction)

My name is … __ __   __ __ __ __ __ …
              14 2   13 13 1 14 4

A pleasure. __ __ __ __ __ __ __ __ __
             2 15 7 1 15 21 1 8 4

24. La cortesía (Politeness)

Thank you very much.   ___ ___ ___ ___ ___ ___   ___ ___ ___ ___ ___ ___ ___
                              14 5 7 11 1 20   10 19 1 7 3 1 20

You're welcome.   ___ ___   ___ ___ ___ ___
                       8 2   15 1 8 1

25. Más cortesía (More Politeness)

Have a good trip!   ¡___ ___ ___ ___   ___ ___ ___ ___ ___!
                    6 5 2 15   22 3 1 12 2

Congratulations!   ¡___ ___ ___ ___ ___ ___ ___ ___ ___ ___ ___ ___ ___ ___!
                9 2 13 3 7 3 21 1 7 3 4 15 2 20

The puzzles in this section are just a bit harder than the ones in the previous section. The types of clues that you are given to solve them are similar, but a little trickier. You will be given hints, but fewer than in the previous section.

CRUCIGRAMAS (CROSSWORDS)
La comida (Food)

26. Las verduras (Vegetables)

Horizontales	Verticales
1. Avocado	2. Pea
6. Asparagus	3. Eggplant
	4. Spinach

Horizontales (continúa)

8.

11. Olive

12.

13.

14.

16. Carrot

17.

Verticales (continúa)

5.

7.

9.

10.

15.

27. Las frutas (Fruits)

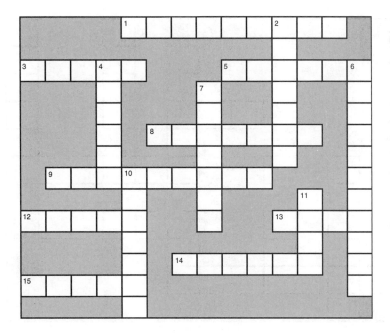

Horizontales

1.

3. Strawberry

5. Cherry

8.

9. Raspberry

12.

13. Fig

14.

15. Melon

Verticales

2. Grapefruit

4. Watermelon

6. Apricot

7.

10.

11. Pineapple

28. La carne (Meat)

Horizontales

4.

7. Liver

8. Pork

9. Veal

Verticales

1. Turkey

2. Bacon

3.

5.

6.

29. El pescado y el marisco (Fish and Seafood)

Horizontales

1.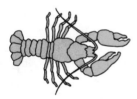

4. Clam

6.

8. Codfish

10. Mussels

12. Trout

13. Herring

Verticales

2. Anchovy

3. Squids

5.

(singular)

7. Salmon

9.

11. Tuna

30. Comidas diversas (Diverse Foods)

Horizontales

4. Rice

5. Sugar

7. Margarine

9. Pepper

11. Cream

13.

15.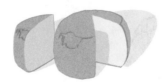

16. Mustard

17.

18. Pie

Verticales

1. Yogurt

2. Salt

3. Cookie

6.

8. Noodles

10.

12. Vinegar

14.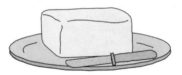

16. Honey

Términos opuestos: Adverbios, adjetivos, sustantivos y verbos (Opposites: Adverbs, Adjectives, Nouns, and Verbs)

31. Los adverbios (Adverbs)

Horizontales	Verticales
2. Never	1. Late
4. Always	3. Early
5. Slowly	
6. Fast	

32. Más adverbios (More Adverbs)

Horizontales

3. Nearby
6. Below

Verticales

1. Far away
2. Inside
4. Above
5. Outside

33. Los adjetivos (Adjectives)

Horizontales

4. Young
6. Ugly
7. Tall
8. Beautiful

Verticales

1. Fat
2. Slender
3. Old
5. Short

34. Los sustantivos (Nouns)

Horizontales

2. Child
3. Adult
5. Woman

Verticales

1. Man
2. Night
4. Day

35. Los verbos (Verbs)

Horizontales

1. To remember
5. To lose
7. To find
8. To forget

Verticales

2. To hate
3. To love
4. To live
6. To die

El comer y el beber (Eating and Drinking)

36. Las bebidas (Drinks)

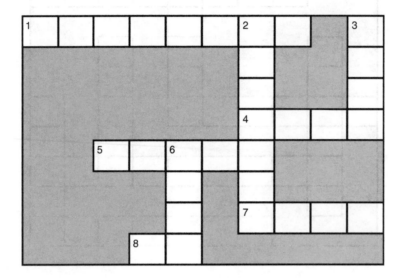

Horizontales

1. Soft drink

4. Wine

5.

7.

8. Tea

Verticales

2.

3. Juice

6.

37. En un restaurante (At a Restaurant)

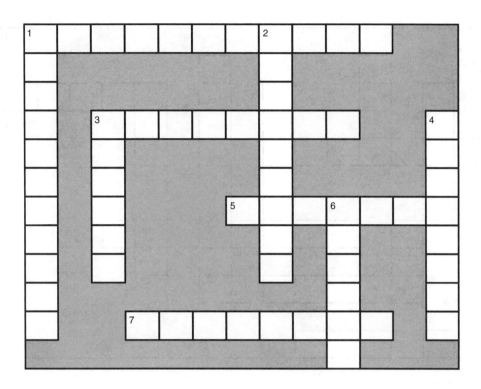

Horizontales

1. Reservation
3. Waitress
5. Tip
7. Service

Verticales

1. Restaurant
2. Cafeteria
3. Bill, check
4. Waiter
6. Price

38. ¡Vamos a comer! (Let's Eat!)

Horizontales

7   To cost

8. To have lunch

10. To have a snack

11. To toast

12. To serve

Verticales

1. To order

2. To pour

3. To have dinner

4. To have breakfast

5. To eat

6. To cut

7. To cook

9. To drink

39. Las descripciones (Descriptions)

Horizontales

1. Salty
3. Bad
6. Hot (warm)
8. Fried
9. Spicy
10. Sour
11. Cold

Verticales

2. Sweet
4. Appetizing
5. Tasty
7. Good

40. Las expresiones (Expressions)

Horizontales

2. Course, dish
6. Tray
7. Menu
8. Pitcher

Verticales

1. Portion
3. Thirst
4. Cheers!
5. Hunger

PALABRAS ESCONDIDAS (WORD SEARCH)

Las ciudades, el tráfico y los lugares
(Cities, Traffic, and Places)

The hidden words can be read horizontally, vertically, and diagonally, in any direction.

41. Las ciudades (Cities)

D	L	E	T	N	E	U	F	M
W	A	K	M	T	L	A	O	O
P	L	D	N	M	P	F	I	N
M	A	E	U	U	B	U	C	U
R	U	R	E	I	L	E	I	M
P	N	B	Q	P	C	R	F	E
M	L	L	N	U	T	A	I	N
O	Q	Z	R	P	E	S	D	T
C	A	P	I	T	A	L	E	O

Suburbs   __ __ __ __ __ __ __

Capital   __ __ __ __ __ __ __

City   __ __ __ __ __ __

Building   __ __ __ __ __ __ __ __

Fountain   __ __ __ __ __ __

Monument   __ __ __ __ __ __ __ __ __

Park   __ __ __ __ __ __

Town   __ __ __ __ __ __

Bridge   __ __ __ __ __ __

42. El tráfico (Traffic)

```
R   A   C   A   T   A   S   C   O
M   C   O   D   C   T   H   E   R
Q   C   N   M   Y   Y   H   A   O
S   I   D   Q   X   C   R   D   F
A   D   U   G   O   T   J   A   Á
L   E   C   C   H   M   L   R   M
I   N   T   X   K   R   R   T   E
D   T   O   G   Q   H   Y   N   S
A   E   R   N   J   C   M   E   G
```

Accident   __ __ __ __ __ __ __ __

Traffic jam __ __ __ __ __ __ __

Car   __ __ __ __ __

Driver   __ __ __ __ __ __ __ __ __

Entrance   __ __ __ __ __ __ __

Exit   __ __ __ __ __ __

Traffic light __ __ __ __ __ __ __ __

43. Las calles (Streets)

```
P  N  T  C  J  N  N  N  A  B
F  K  E  L  N  Q  T  D  X  O
Z  R  R  S  T  N  I  T  C  C
E  L  X  Q  Q  N  K  E  J  A
L  Y  G  Y  E  U  N  M  W  C
L  F  Q  V  L  T  I  K  R  A
A  M  A  J  R  M  K  N  V  L
C  Y  T  O  G  Z  M  R  A  L
F  F  L  Y  M  G  C  D  T  E
V  C  A  R  R  E  T  E  R  A
```

Avenue   __ __ __ __ __ __ __

Intersection __ __ __ __ __ __ __ __ __

Street   __ __ __ __ __

Highway   __ __ __ __ __ __ __ __ __

Downtown   __ __ __ __ __ __

Corner   __ __ __ __ __ __

44. Los edificios (Buildings)

```
R  O  L  R  F  R  N  D  P  O  A
C  B  E  T  R  V  B  F  T  C  P
O  C  V  S  C  A  S  A  E  N  A
R  M  I  Y  U  B  N  T  Q  A  Z
R  F  J  N  T  M  O  E  D  B  A
E  P  N  K  E  I  S  N  H  T  L
O  Q  M  W  L  C  E  Q  P  X  P
R  N  P  B  U  I  Y  B  Y  Z  L
Z  Y  I  E  T  R  C  R  L  N  J
P  B  L  C  Q  B  R  H  H  J  N
N  A  Q  T  A  I  S  E  L  G  I
```

Bank   __ __ __ __ __

Library   __ __ __ __ __ __ __ __ __ __

House   __ __ __ __ __

Movie theater   __ __ __ __

Post office   __ __ __ __ __ __

School   __ __ __ __ __ __ __

Church   __ __ __ __ __ __ __

Museum   __ __ __ __ __

Town square   __ __ __ __ __

Store   __ __ __ __ __ __

45. Los lugares (Places)

```
K  T  E  M  P  L  O  K  P  O
M  P  O  N  K  W  R  T  R  I
N  H  L  R  C  B  T  N  W  R
F  T  R  P  R  O  A  L  N  A
H  M  G  T  I  E  E  R  F  N
K  M  B  R  J  J  T  N  T  A
X  J  R  K  N  J  I  P  H  P
N  A  L  Q  V  G  F  L  K  M
B  J  P  T  X  K  N  Q  B  A
F  J  J  H  R  L  A  B  Q  C
```

Amphitheater   __ __ __ __ __ __ __ __ __ __

Neighborhood   __ __ __ __ __ __

Bell tower   __ __ __ __ __ __ __ __ __ __

Temple   __ __ __ __ __ __

Tower   __ __ __ __ __

CRIPTOGRAMAS (CRYPTOGRAMS)
La etiqueta y la cortesía (Manners and Politeness)

A specific letter will correspond to another letter in the cryptograms below. For example, if you establish that Z corresponds to A in any of the five puzzles, you can go ahead and substitute that letter for each occurrence of the alphabetic letter Z in the remaining puzzles. In addition to the Z = A correspondence, the following are two additional alphabetic correlations: The code letter X = D, and the code letter D = I.

46. La etiqueta (Manners)

Good day!

¡Y P B S G I   X D Z I !

Don't mention it.

S G   U Z O   X B   H P B .

47. La cortesía (Politeness)

Excuse me!

¡A G S   R B Q F D I G !

Pardon me!

¡R B Q X G S !

48. El viaje (Travel)

Have a good holiday!

¡H P B   R Z I B   Y P B S Z I

L Z A Z A D G S B I !

Have a nice time!

¡X D L D B Q J Z I B !

49. El acuerdo y el desacuerdo (Agreement and Disagreement)

Of course!

¡ _ _ _ _ _   _ _ _   _ _ !
¡ A T Z Q G   H P B   I D !

I don't believe it!

¡ _ _   _ _   _ _ _ _ _
¡ S G   T G   R P B X G

_ _ _ _ _ !
A Q B B Q !

50. Las expresiones diversas (Diverse Expressions)

Bless you! (after a sneeze)

¡ _ _ _ _ _ !
¡ I Z T P X !

Come in!

¡ _ _ _ _   _ _ _ _ _ !
¡ R Z I B   P I J B X !

Tough Puzzles

The puzzles in this section are harder than the ones you have been solving so far, but not much more. The types of clues you are given to solve them are just a little tougher. As always, have fun!

CRUCIGRAMAS (CROSSWORDS)

El trabajo y las carreras
(Work and Careers)

51. El trabajo (Work)

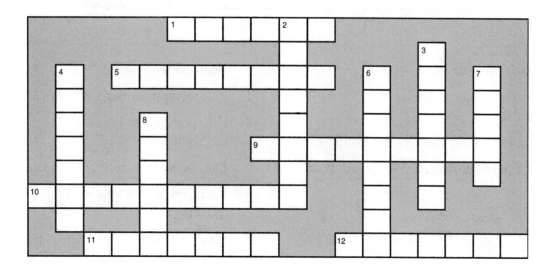

Horizontales	Verticales
1. Esta persona trabaja con personas enfermas.	2. Esta persona trabaja en un restaurante.
5. Esta persona repara automóviles.	3. Esta persona combate fuegos.
9. Esta persona trabaja con el cabello de otra persona.	4. Esta persona enseña a los estudiantes.
10. Esta persona crea y construye edificios.	6. Esta persona trabaja en un banco.
11. Esta persona da consejos legales.	7. Esta persona trabaja en televisión y en películas.
12. Esta persona protege al público.	8. Esta persona toca instrumentos musicales.

52. Más trabajo (More Work)

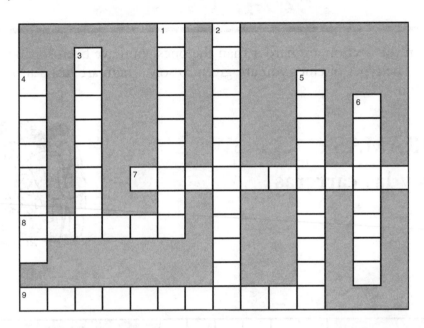

Horizontales

7. Esta persona escribe artículos para un periódico.
8. Esta persona trabaja en las fábricas.
9. Esta persona trabaja con los animales.

Verticales

1. Esta persona trabaja con la carne.
2. Esta persona trabaja con la electricidad.
3. Esta persona vende cosas a otros.
4. Esta persona enseña en una universidad.
5. Esta persona trabaja con la madera para construir casas.
6. Esta persona trabaja con los dientes de otra persona.

53. En la oficina (At the Office)

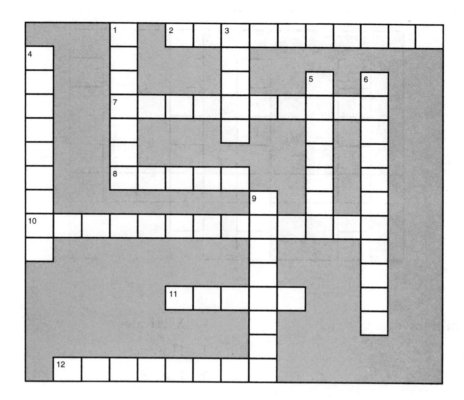

Horizontales

2.

7. Desk

8. Chair

10. Photocopier

11.

12. Telephone

Verticales

1. Scissors

3. Pencil

4.

5. File

6. Computer

9.

54. Los lugares de trabajo (Workplaces)

Horizontales

5. Library

Verticales

1. Hospital

2. Factory

3. Office

4. Stock exchange

55. **El trabajo** (Working)

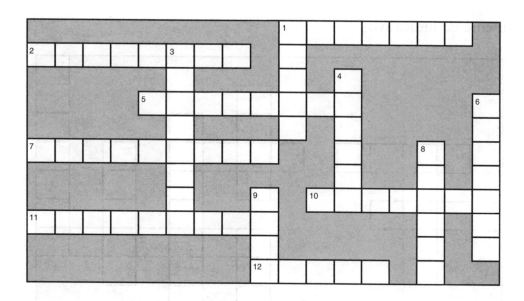

Horizontales

1. Manager
2. Commerce
5. Employee
7. To hire
10. Career
11. To retire (oneself)
12. To fire

Verticales

1. To earn
3. Company
4. Work associate
6. Work
8. Salary
9. Boss

Los verbos (Verbs)

56. El presente de indicativo (The Present Indicative)

Horizontales

4. You (*usted*) do open
6. You (*usted*) are dining
8. You (*usted*) ought/should
9. You (*tú*) chat
10. I write
11. You (*tú*) leave (*salir*)

Verticales

1. We live
2. You (*tú*) are reading
3. We sing
5. We are drinking
7. I speak
9. I eat

57. El presente de indicativo: los verbos irregulares
(Present Indicative: Irregular Verbs)

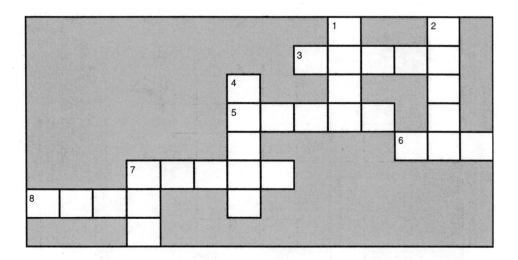

Horizontales

3. I fall
5. I am (*estar*)
6. I am (*ser*)
7. I come
8. I say

Verticales

1. I do
2. I put
4. I have
7. I go

58. El presente de indicativo: más verbos irregulares
(The Present Indicative: More Irregular Verbs)

Horizontales	Verticales
4. I close	1. I die
5. I hear	2. I play (*jugar*)
7. I return (*volver*)	3. I bring
9. I know (*conocer*)	4. I drive
10. I give	6. I order (*pedir*)
	8. I see

59. El imperfecto de indicativo (Imperfect Indicative)

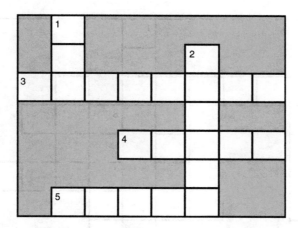

Horizontales

3. They were talking
4. You (*usted*) were eating
5. You (*tú*) were seeing

Verticales

1. I was (*ser*)
2. We were going

60. El pretérito (Preterit)

Horizontales

3. He was (*estar*)
6. He went
7. He ate
8. He did
9. He came
10. He had
11. He said

Verticales

1. He gave
2. He spoke
3. He wrote
4. He returned (*volver*)
5. He put
7. He drove

El recreo y los deportes (Recreation and Sports)

61. Los deportes (Sports)

Horizontales

3.

7. Volleyball

8.

9. Soccer

11.

Verticales

1.

2. Boxing

4.

5. Baseball

6.

10. Tennis

62. Los edificios (Buildings)

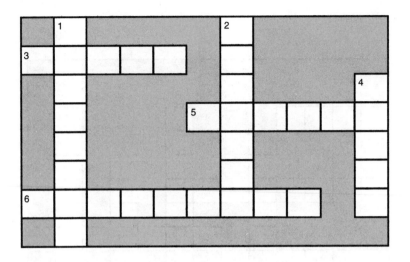

Horizontales

3. Place to compete in track and field.
5. Place to play basketball.
6. Place where horses race.

Verticales

1. Place where gymnasts practice.
2. Place to play sports such as soccer.
4. Place to play baseball.

63. Los instrumentos deportivos (Sports Equipment)

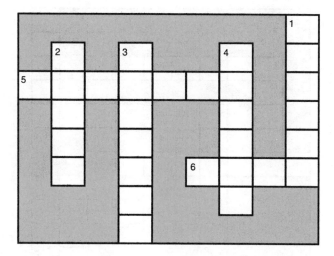

Horizontales

5. Tennis racket
6. Bowling ball

Verticales

1. Baseball
2. Dice
3. Gloves (boxing, baseball)
4. Darts

64. El ocio (Leisure Time)

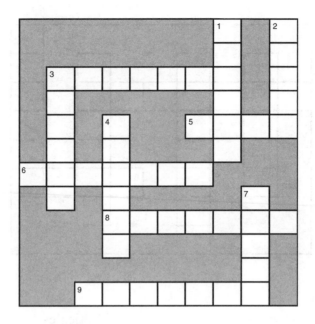

Horizontales	Verticales
3. To walk	1. To run
5. To read	2. To play
6. To skate	3. To sing
8. To camp	4. To dance
9. To ski	7. To swim

65. Las diversiones (Entertainment)

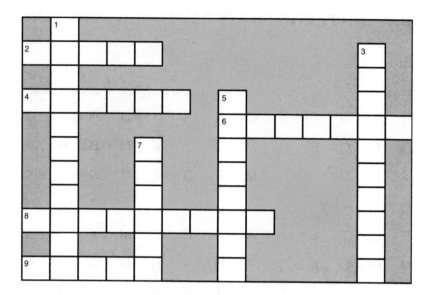

Horizontales

2. Game
4. Billiards
6. Chess
8. Stamp collecting
9. Checkers

Verticales

1. Coin collecting
3. Video game
5. Swimming
7. Playing cards

PALABRAS ESCONDIDAS (WORD SEARCH)
La salud y las emergencias (Health and Emergencies)

66. En el hospital (At the Hospital)

```
R  N  B  R  V  O  N  A  J  U  R  I  C
D  F  O  E  O  M  D  T  X  M  B  N  A
A  G  C  C  I  M  É  D  I  C  O  R  K
D  T  I  E  P  H  C  P  T  Y  E  L  K
E  E  T  L  O  W  O  Z  X  M  X  H  K
M  R  Ó  A  C  A  N  S  R  G  C  M  P
R  M  I  V  S  R  T  E  P  C  X  A  H
E  Ó  B  N  O  P  F  E  W  I  C  C  N
F  M  I  O  T  N  Z  R  C  I  T  H  M
N  E  T  C  E  V  V  L  E  E  K  A  L
E  T  N  N  T  F  R  N  V  H  R  Y  L
N  R  A  R  S  J  T  J  V  M  K  C  M
T  O  L  R  E  E  D  Q  Y  G  N  R  Z
```

Antibiotic   — — — — — — — — — — —

Surgeon   — — — — — — — — —

To convalesce   — — — — — — — — — — —

Illness   — — — — — — — — —

Nurse   — — — — — — — —

Stethoscope   — — — — — — — — — — — — —

Hospital   — — — — — — — —

Doctor   — — — — — —

Patient   — — — — — — — —

Prescription   — — — — — —

Thermometer   — — — — — — — — — — —

67. El médico (The Doctor)

```
F   M   W   A   N   I   R   I   P   S   A   A
E   N   F   E   R   M   O   P   P   H   J   R
D   O   L   E   R   R   B   A   H   E   D   U
X   M   Y   L   O   W   D   F   R   P   G   C
H   R   E   L   O   E   Q   B   Z   A   K   M
M   I   O   D   C   S   E   J   R   S   N   V
Y   D   N   E   I   I   L   G   V   T   A   O
M   H   R   C   F   C   A   U   R   I   D   M
Z   R   F   K   H   N   I   R   P   L   N   I
M   C   N   N   T   A   S   N   Y   L   E   T
C   Q   T   A   K   C   D   O   A   A   V   A
S   O   I   V   R   E   N   O   T   F   F   R
```

Aspirin	__ __ __ __ __ __ __ __
Cure	__ __ __ __
To hurt	__ __ __ __ __
Ache	__ __ __ __ __
Sick	__ __ __ __ __ __ __
Fever	__ __ __ __ __ __
Throat	__ __ __ __ __ __ __ __
Swollen	__ __ __ __ __ __ __ __
Medicine	__ __ __ __ __ __ __ __ __
Nerves	__ __ __ __ __ __ __
To suffer	__ __ __ __ __ __ __
Tablet	__ __ __ __ __ __ __ __
Pulse	__ __ __ __ __
Cough	__ __ __
Bandage	__ __ __ __ __
To throw up	__ __ __ __ __ __ __ __

68. El dentista (The Dentist)

```
N  N  M  D  W  Z  R  H  M  G  K  B  E
K  C  E  P  I  L  L  A  R  S  E  T  T
F  E  X  A  M  I  N  A  R  C  R  D  N
C  A  J  U  G  A  H  E  Z  I  R  E  E
N  O  K  J  N  V  I  N  P  Z  M  N  U
X  H  R  N  Y  R  M  U  T  R  M  T  P
M  F  J  O  A  C  C  A  R  C  L  I  C
B  M  X  C  N  S  L  U  M  M  R  S  I
A  P  T  G  E  A  R  G  V  U  K  T  T
B  C  C  H  D  I  E  N  T  E  E  A  A
F  K  O  R  P  R  D  E  Z  N  P  L  R
L  T  O  B  R  J  R  L  T  J  N  Q  A
R  F  N  P  F  L  Q  G  P  G  R  N  L
```

Needle   — — — — —

Mouth   — — — —

Cavity   — — — — —

To brush oneself — — — — — — — — — —

Appointment   — — — —

Crown   — — — — — —

Dentist   — — — — — — — —

Tooth   — — — — — —

To spit   — — — — — — —

To examine   — — — — — — — —

Tongue   — — — — — —

Molar   — — — — —

Bridge   — — — — — —

Drill   — — — — — —

69. Las enfermedades (Ailments)

A	A	Í	N	O	M	L	U	P	V	N
P	D	I	N	F	E	C	C	I	Ó	N
E	E	R	R	Y	J	D	K	H	M	K
N	P	R	E	S	F	R	I	A	D	O
D	R	Ú	A	V	L	D	H	L	A	V
I	E	A	L	E	J	D	N	L	E	N
C	S	M	R	C	R	P	E	P	K	R
I	I	S	V	T	E	R	I	G	W	K
T	Ó	A	L	T	G	R	A	M	D	N
I	N	T	T	I	G	B	A	I	L	V
S	L	L	A	T	D	Z	K	D	D	Q

Allergy   __ __ __ __ __ __ __ __

Appendicitis __ __ __ __ __ __ __ __ __ __ __ __

Asthma   __ __ __ __

Depression   __ __ __ __ __ __ __ __ __ __

Diarrhea   __ __ __ __ __ __ __ __

Flu   __ __ __ __ __

Infection   __ __ __ __ __ __ __ __ __

Pneumonia   __ __ __ __ __ __ __ __

Cold   __ __ __ __ __ __ __ __ __

Ulcer   __ __ __ __ __ __

70. Las emergencias (Emergencies)

```
B  P  E  L  I  G  R  O  L  A  A
B  C  F  B  C  S  F  O  A  M  I
K  A  K  U  A  P  R  F  R  B  C
L  J  L  N  E  R  K  R  U  U  N
K  K  G  L  O  G  M  R  D  L  E
H  R  G  C  I  L  O  D  A  A  G
E  K  O  Z  V  M  N  Q  M  N  R
Q  S  N  P  G  T  A  H  E  C  E
A  D  I  R  E  H  Y  C  U  I  M
R  E  S  C  A  T  A  R  Q  A  E
B  A  C  C  I  D  E  N  T  E  G
```

Accident   __ __ __ __ __ __ __ __ __

Ambulance   __ __ __ __ __ __ __ __ __ __

Stretcher   __ __ __ __ __ __ __

Emergency   __ __ __ __ __ __ __ __ __ __

Fire   __ __ __ __ __

Injury   __ __ __ __ __ __

Danger   __ __ __ __ __ __ __

Burn   __ __ __ __ __ __ __ __

To rescue   __ __ __ __ __ __ __ __

Blood   __ __ __ __ __ __

Help!   __ __ __ __ __ __ __

CRUCIGRAMAS (CROSSWORDS)

El aspecto, el ánimo y el intelecto
(Appearance, Mood, and Intellect)

71. El salón de belleza (The Beauty Parlor)

Horizontales	Verticales
1. Beautician, hairdresser	2. To wash
4. Barber shop	3. To brush oneself
8. To dry	5. To trim
9. Beauty shop	6. Barber
10. To cut	7. To clean
11. To comb oneself	

72. Los productos de belleza (Beauty Products)

Horizontales

1.

4. Shampoo

7. Hair

9.

11. Makeup

12. Hair spray

13.

14. Brush

Verticales

2. Mascara

3.

5. Touch up

6. Permanent

8.

10. Rinse

73. El ánimo (Mood)

Horizontales

1. Indecisive
5. Irritable
8. Angry
9. Sad
10. Impulsive

Verticales

2. Affectionate
3. Sensitive
4. Jealous
6. Happy
7. Anxious

74. La intelecto (Intellect)

Horizontales

1. Intelligent
5. Smart
6. Wise
7. Idiot

Verticales

2. Stupid
3. Genius
4. Fool

75. La personalidad (Personality)

Horizontales

3. Generous
9. Outgoing
10. Shy
11. Reserved

Verticales

1. Stubborn
2. Aggressive
4. Nice
5. Sincere
6. Funny
7. Unpleasant
8. Friendly

Challenging Puzzles

The puzzles in this section are the hardest of this book, but certainly not impossible to do. The clues require you to use a little more thinking, and, maybe, require background research.

CRUCIGRAMAS (CROSSWORDS)

La flora y la fauna (Flora and Fauna)

76. Los animales (Animals)

Horizontales	Verticales
2.	1. 

Horizontales (continúa)

6.

8. Lamb

9. Rabbit

10.

11.

13. Camel

16. Fox

17.

18. Bull

20. Ox

Verticales (continúa)

3. Pig

4. Bat

5. Animal

7.

9.

12.

13. Goat (female)

14. Dog

15.

19.

77. Las aves (Birds)

Horizontales

2. Parrot
4.
5.
6. Pigeon
7.
11. Owl
14. Seagull
15.
16. Nightingale
17. Parakeet

18.

Verticales

1. Sparrow
3. Ostrich
6. Pelican
8. Vulture
9.
10. Bird
12. Goose
13.

78. Los peces (Fish)

[Crossword grid]

Horizontales	**Verticales**
3. Eel	1. Toad
4. 	2. Salamander
	4. 
9. Frog	5. Seal
10. Dolphin	6. Sardine
11. 	7. 
12. Whale	8. Reptile

79. Los árboles (Trees)

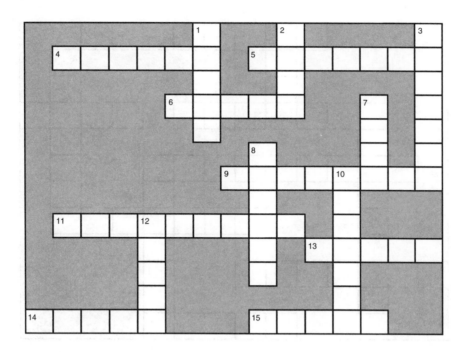

Horizontales	Verticales
4. Cherry tree	1. Oak tree
5. Fig tree	2. Pine tree
6. Poplar tree	3. Apple tree
9. Lemon tree	7. Maple tree
11. Peach tree	8. Cypress
13. Palm tree	10. Orange tree
14. Olive tree	12. Fir tree
15. Tree	

80. Las flores (Flowers)

Horizontales

1. Orchid

4.

5. Flower

6. Daisy

8. Petunia

9.

10.

Verticales

2.

3.

4. Gladiolus

7.

Las definiciones (Definitions)

81. Los verbos (Verbs)

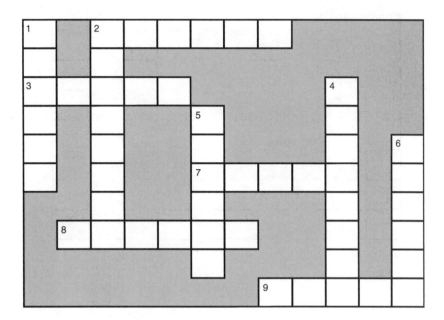

<table>
<tr><td>

Horizontales

2. Producir sonidos con una voz rítmica y modulada.

3. Poseer algo.

7. Tocar los labios de otra persona como señal de amor.

8. Llamar en voz alta.

9. Fijar la vista en una cosa o persona, observar.

</td><td>

Verticales

1. Pasar por una puerta de fuera a adentro.

2. Manejar un coche.

4. Representar palabras, números e ideas por medio de símbolos.

5. Usar palabras para expresarse a otra persona.

6. Hacer un viaje.

</td></tr>
</table>

82. Más verbos (More Verbs)

Horizontales

2. Dar una cosa o servicio a alguien por dinero.

4. Representar personas u objetos en una superficie con colores.

6. Representar con un lápiz en una superficie.

7. Comer el almuerzo.

Verticales

1. Comer el desayuno.

3. Pagar dinero a alguien por una cosa o servicio.

5. Comer la cena.

83. Aún más verbos (Even More Verbs)

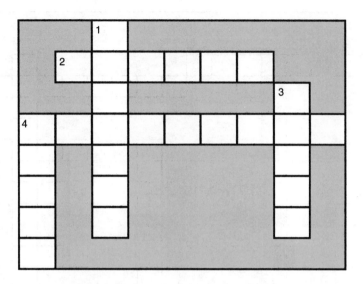

Horizontales

2. El perro se puso a . . .
4. El caballo se puso a . . .

Verticales

1. El gato se puso a . . .
3. El oveja se puso a . . .
4. El león se puso a . . .

84. Los adjetivos (Adjectives)

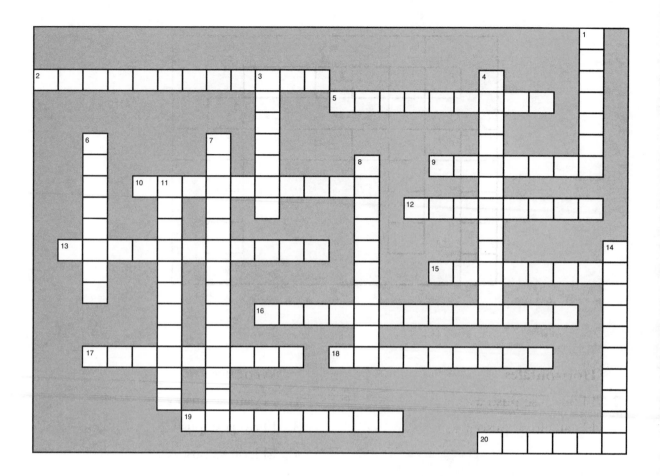

Horizontales

2. Una persona de Guatemala.
5. Una persona de Argentina.
9. Una persona de Perú.
10. Una persona de Venezuela.
12. Una persona de Uruguay.
13. Una persona de El Salvador.
15. Una persona de Panamá.
16. Una persona de Costa Rica.
17. Una persona de Paraguay.
18. Una persona de Honduras.
19. Una persona de Bolivia.
20. Una persona de Cuba.

Verticales

1. Una persona de Chile.
3. Una persona de España.
4. Una persona de Nicaragua.
6. Una persona de México.
7. Una persona de Puerto Rico.
8. Una persona de La República Dominicana.
11. Una persona de Ecuador.
14. Una persona de Colombia.

85. Los sustantivos (Nouns)

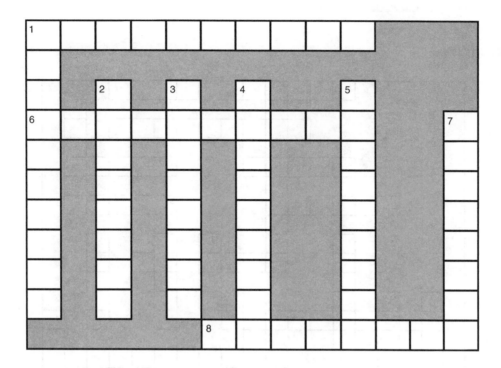

Horizontales

1. Una tienda donde se venden los pasteles y las tortas.

6. Una tienda donde se vende la carne.

8. Una tienda donde se venden los medicamentos.

Verticales

1. Una tienda donde se venden el pescado y el marisco.

2. Una tienda donde se vende la fruta.

3. Una tienda donde se venden los libros.

4. Una tienda donde se vende el helado.

5. Una tienda donde se vende el pan.

7. Una tienda donde se venden los productos lácteos.

El viaje y el transporte público
(Travel and Public Transportation)

86. **Los coches** (Cars)

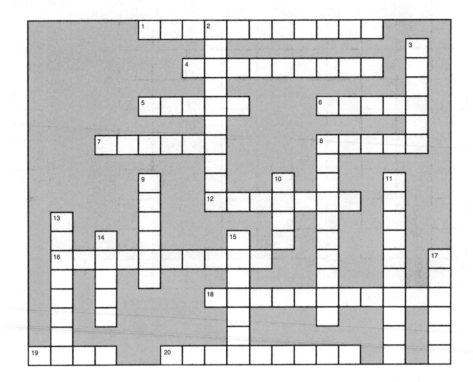

Horizontales

1. Bumper
4.
5. Lights
6. Motor, engine
7. Horn
8. License plate
12. To repair
16.

18. Heating
19. Hood
20. Ignition

Verticales

2.

3. Door
8. Windshield
9. Gas tank
10. Trunk
11. Car window

13. Glove compartment
14.

15. Steering wheel
17. Handle

87. Los aeropuertos y los aviones (Airports and Planes)

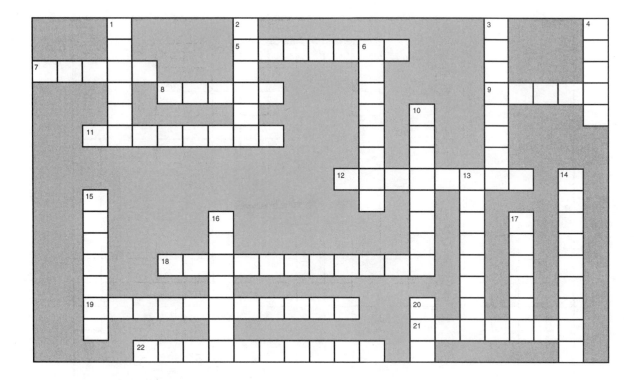

Horizontales

5. Flight attendant
7. Flight
8. To board
9. Runway
11. To check (luggage)
12. Porter
18. Reservation
19. Crew
21. Arrival
22. Airport

Verticales

1. Departure
2. Cabin
3. To take off
4. To fly
6. Terminal
10. Connection
13. Boarding
14. To land
15. Toilet
16. Aisle
17. Gate
20. Wing

88. Los trenes y los autobuses (Trains and Buses)

Horizontales

2. Bus
4. Ticket counter
5. To leave
10. Late
12. Subway
16. Stop
17. Ticket checker
18. Train
19. Railroad

Verticales

1. Bus driver
3. Ticket
6. Seat
7. Early
8. To miss
9. Schedule
11. Platform
13. Track
14. Express
15. Newsstand

89. Los hoteles (Hotels)

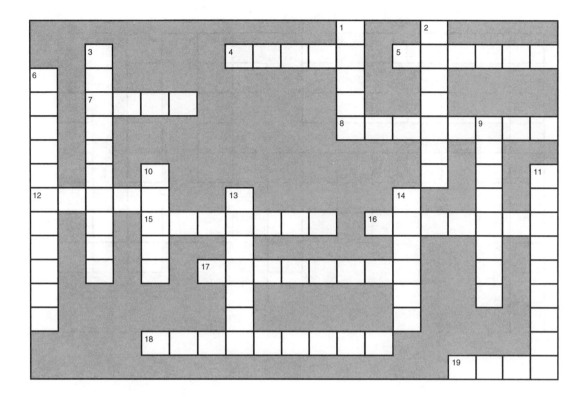

Horizontales

4. Hotel
5. Receipt
7. Bathroom
8. Luggage
12. Shower
15. Manager
16. Bellboy
17. Stairway
18. Reception desk
19. Floor

Verticales

1. Key
2. Boardinghouse
3. Room
6. Hotel clerk
9. Elevator
10. To pay
11. Lobby
13. Message
14. Inn

90. Las vacaciones (Vacations)

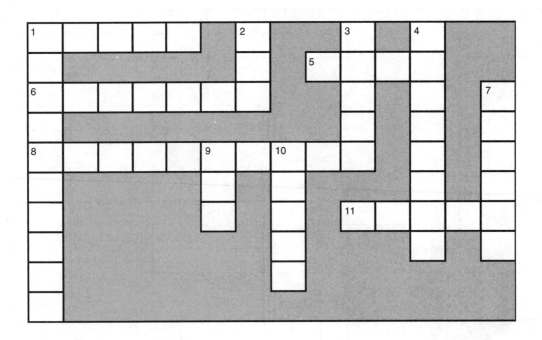

Horizontales

1. Trip
5. Lake
6. Cruise
8. Campground
11. Beach

Verticales

1. Vacations
2. River
3. Ship
4. Mountains
7. To fish
9. Sea
10. To swim

PALABRAS ESCONDIDAS (WORD SEARCH)
Las computadoras y la tecnología
(Computers and Technology)

91. Las computadoras (Computers)

```
R  N  M  A  R  C  H  I  V  O  M  Q  H  J  G  G
O  R  Ó  P  R  O  C  E  S  A  D  O  R  V  G  M
T  A  L  I  C  F  Q  Y  S  F  F  G  M  G  G  I
P  Z  I  G  C  G  W  B  L  C  K  W  V  M  N  K
U  M  R  R  M  N  O  N  B  A  Á  T  G  S  N  Z
R  Ó  E  M  O  C  U  B  Q  R  M  N  T  W  J  C
R  D  R  L  S  M  K  F  A  O  C  A  E  H  A  T
E  E  H  I  B  R  E  M  L  D  L  R  V  R  R  R
T  M  D  K  O  I  A  M  I  A  N  D  D  L  O  M
N  M  D  S  L  R  T  C  R  T  K  V  X  C  S  O
I  R  R  G  F  O  A  R  U  K  M  T  T  E  N
K  U  A  O  L  N  N  K  P  P  J  G  V  N  R  I
C  Q  R  T  O  C  M  M  F  M  F  V  Z  Q  P  T
H  P  Y  M  Ó  M  N  J  D  O  O  M  R  L  M  O
S  O  T  A  D  N  W  M  C  C  Q  C  M  J  I  R
L  Y  M  O  D  A  L  C  E  T  C  N  T  W  Q  M
```

File   __ __ __ __ __ __ __

Compatible   __ __ __ __ __ __ __ __ __ __

Computer   __ __ __ __ __ __ __ __ __ __ __

Cursor   __ __ __ __ __ __

Data   __ __ __ __ __

Disk   — — — — —

Scanner   — — — — — — —

Function   — — — — — — —

Printer   — — — — — — — —

To install   — — — — — — — —

Power switch   — — — — — — — — — —

Memory   — — — — — — —

Monitor   — — — — — — —

Modem   — — — — —

Processor   — — — — — — — — — —

Program   — — — — — — — —

Mouse   — — — — —

Keyboard   — — — — — — —

Icon   — — — — —

92. La televisión (Television)

```
N  N  V  T  C  V  L  P  O  N  E  R
N  Ó  I  H  A  T  R  R  D  T  N  R
R  I  D  L  D  N  Q  J  R  L  O  T
S  S  E  L  E  H  U  A  H  S  W  H
A  I  O  Q  N  G  G  N  I  L  J  B
I  V  C  L  A  A  L  V  C  N  M  M
C  E  A  V  P  Z  E  A  V  I  I  Q
I  L  S  A  C  L  T  Q  N  R  O  Z
T  E  E  X  E  B  Y  M  A  A  L  V
O  T  T  T  K  M  L  R  D  W  C  R
N  Y  E  L  X  E  I  R  E  S  Y  M
T  T  E  L  E  N  O  V  E  L  A  H
```

Commercial   _ _ _ _ _ _ _

To switch off   _ _ _ _ _ _ _

Network   _ _ _ _ _ _

Channel   _ _ _ _ _

To watch   _ _ _ _ _

News   _ _ _ _ _ _ _ _ _

To switch on   _ _ _ _ _

Series   _ _ _ _ _

Soap opera   _ _ _ _ _ _ _ _ _ _

Television   _ _ _ _ _ _ _ _ _ _

Television set   _ _ _ _ _ _ _ _ _

Videocassette   _ _ _ _ _ _ _ _ _ _ _

93. El Internet (Internet)

```
R  O  D  A  G  E  V  A  N  R  L  S  I  T  I  O  F
Q  P  U  E  R  T  O  S  P  L  Y  A  N  T  G  R  P
R  A  R  R  A  N  C  A  R  O  K  R  D  M  N  Q  T
A  E  C  A  L  N  E  R  H  S  T  R  G  X  G  K  M
S  B  N  N  P  H  J  K  R  E  C  A  M  K  J  A  W
E  Z  X  N  M  R  L  M  R  C  K  S  N  G  Ñ  V  A
R  K  Y  M  N  D  A  O  T  C  K  T  V  E  P  C  T
G  K  G  H  X  Y  D  G  Q  A  Z  R  S  N  T  R  F
E  P  M  L  C  A  K  P  E  Z  P  A  J  U  D  D  E
R  D  T  B  C  O  Y  B  H  V  R  R  A  E  E  S  J
O  W  K  R  C  P  N  J  U  T  A  L  R  S  R  E  A
T  D  A  M  R  N  K  E  N  S  I  N  C  F  M  R  S
R  M  A  X  T  T  Q  O  C  Z  C  A  M  V  L  V  N
R  R  L  R  K  K  C  M  A  T  R  A  N  Y  H  I  E
M  L  K  R  F  K  H  R  L  G  A  F  D  P  R  D  M
Y  M  N  B  T  I  W  D  A  V  K  R  L  O  M  O  D
P  T  P  F  D  K  C  R  R  X  T  G  N  R  R  R  J
```

Access   __ __ __ __ __ __

To upgrade   __ __ __ __ __ __ __ __ __ __ __

To boot   __ __ __ __ __ __ __ __ __

To drag   __ __ __ __ __ __ __ __ __ __

Search engine   __ __ __ __ __ __ __ __ __

Encrypted   __ __ __ __ __ __ __ __

To connect   __ __ __ __ __ __ __ __

Password   __ __ __ __ __ __ __ __ __ __

To download   __ __ __ __ __ __ __ __ __

Link   __ __ __ __ __ __

Bookmark   __ __ __ __ __ __ __ __

Message   __ __ __ __ __ __ __

Web browser   __ __ __ __ __ __ __ __ __

To surf   __ __ __ __ __ __ __

Ports   __ __ __ __ __ __

Net   __ __ __

To go back   __ __ __ __ __ __ __

Server   __ __ __ __ __ __ __

Site   __ __ __ __ __

94. Las comunicaciones (Communication)

```
O  R  Y  F  A  D  X  M  T  D  T  K
N  O  O  A  U  R  L  W  N  Y  H  B
O  T  C  R  R  O  A  F  C  A  C  Z
F  C  I  O  I  D  M  C  L  L  O  T
Ó  E  R  D  C  A  C  I  O  V  T  K
R  Y  B  A  U  Z  P  A  A  T  G  V
C  O  M  I  L  I  N  T  S  R  J  B
I  R  Á  P  A  N  L  K  A  E  R  G
M  P  L  O  R  A  L  B  Y  G  T  X
Y  Y  A  C  E  G  A  M  K  Y  W  E
T  K  N  V  S  R  T  O  I  D  A  R
N  T  I  Z  F  O  A  N  T  E  N  A
```

Speaker   __ __ __ __ __ __ __

Antenna   __ __ __ __ __ __

Headphones   __ __ __ __ __ __ __ __ __ __ __

Cassette   __ __ __ __ __ __ __

Copier   __ __ __ __ __ __ __ __ __

To record   __ __ __ __ __ __

Wireless   __ __ __ __ __ __ __ __ __ __

Microphone   __ __ __ __ __ __ __ __ __

Organizer   __ __ __ __ __ __ __ __ __ __ __

Battery   __ __ __ __

Projector   __ __ __ __ __ __ __ __ __

Radio   __ __ __ __ __

To play a recording   __ __ __ __ __

95. El teléfono (The telephone)

```
R  R  K  H  M  J  R  Q  N  R  N
R  R  W  Z  N  W  M  P  A  Z  Ó
R  W  W  C  C  D  R  T  V  T  I
A  Y  N  L  N  O  S  H  M  T  C
N  C  W  Z  Q  E  L  P  Z  T  A
O  N  P  G  T  T  M  G  F  L  M
S  F  K  N  X  V  N  R  A  V  R
K  V  O  M  T  L  M  A  B  R  O
P  C  Q  J  X  P  Z  T  K  Y  F
Q  M  A  R  C  A  R  I  Y  W  N
L  A  S  T  E  R  I  S  C  O  I
```

Star   __ __ __ __ __ __ __ __ __

To hang up   __ __ __ __ __ __

To answer   __ __ __ __ __ __ __ __ __

Toll-free   __ __ __ __ __ __

Information   __ __ __ __ __ __ __ __ __ __ __

To dial   __ __ __ __ __ __

To ring   __ __ __ __ __

CRIPTOGRAMS (CRYPTOGRAMS)

La cultura hispana (Hispanic Culture)

A specific letter will correspond to another letter in the cryptograms below. For example, if you establish that Z corresponds to A in any of the five puzzles, you can go ahead and substitute that letter for each occurrence of the letter Z in the remaining puzzles. In addition to the Z = A correspondence, the following are two additional alphabetic correlations: The code letter X = D, and the code letter D = I.

96. Los escritores (Writers)

This Spanish author (1547–1616) wrote Don Quijote. His first name was Miguel.

$$\overline{\text{A}}\ \overline{\text{B}}\ \overline{\text{Q}}\ \overline{\text{L}}\ \overline{\text{Z}}\ \overline{\text{S}}\ \overline{\text{J}}\ \overline{\text{B}}\ \overline{\text{I}}$$

This Colombian author (1928–) wrote *One Hundred Years of Solitude*. He won the Nobel Prize in (1982), and his first name is Gabriel.

$$\overline{\text{C}}\ \overline{\text{Z}}\ \overline{\text{Q}}\ \overline{\text{A}}\ \overline{\text{D}}\ \overline{\text{Z}}\qquad\overline{\text{F}}\ \overline{\text{Z}}\ \overline{\text{Q}}\ \overline{\text{H}}\ \overline{\text{P}}\ \overline{\text{B}}\ \overline{\text{N}}$$

97. Los artistas (Artists)

This Spanish artist (1881–1973) is well known for his abstract paintings. His first name is Pablo.

$$\overline{\text{R}}\ \overline{\text{D}}\ \overline{\text{A}}\ \overline{\text{Z}}\ \overline{\text{I}}\ \overline{\text{I}}\ \overline{\text{G}}$$

This Mexican artist (1907–1954) had a film made about her life. The title of the film used her first name, Frida.

$$\overline{\text{W}}\ \overline{\text{Z}}\ \overline{\text{U}}\ \overline{\text{T}}\ \overline{\text{G}}$$

98. Los músicos (Musicians)

This singer (1957–) was born in Cuba. Her first name is Gloria.

B I J B V Z S

This singer was born in 1947. He won many grammies for his music. His first name is Carlos.

I Z S J Z S Z

99. Las películas (Movies)

This film is about the singer (1941–1959) who died in a plane crash in Iowa. His most famous song is the title of this film.

T Z   Y Z F Y Z

This actress is of Spanish heritage (1974–). Her movies include *Vanilla Sky*. Her first name is Penelope.

A Q P N

100. La cultura popular (Popular Culture)

Antonio was born in Spain in 1960. He acted in Spanish movies and later became a Hollywood star.

$$\overline{\text{Y}}\ \overline{\text{Z}}\ \overline{\text{S}}\ \overline{\text{X}}\ \overline{\text{B}}\ \overline{\text{Q}}\ \overline{\text{Z}}\ \overline{\text{I}}$$

This person is one of the highest paid baseball players (1975–). His first name is Alejandro.

$$\overline{\text{Q}}\ \overline{\text{G}}\ \overline{\text{X}}\ \overline{\text{Q}}\ \overline{\text{D}}\ \overline{\text{C}}\ \overline{\text{P}}\ \overline{\text{B}}\ \overline{\text{N}}$$

Answers

1.

- PARED
- SÓTANO
- ALCOBA
- COCINA
- SALA
- DESPACHO
- ARMARIO
- COMEDOR
- PUERTA
- VENTANA
- DESPENSA
- TECHO
- CASA
- SUELO

2.

- SALERO
- PIMENTERO
- MESA
- CUCHARA
- SERVILLETA
- BOTELLA
- PLATO
- CAFETERA
- PLATILLO
- TETERA
- TENEDOR
- CUCHILLO
- MANTEL

3.

- CAJÓN
- MUEBLE
- LÁMPARA
- ESCRITORIO
- CAMA
- SILLÓN
- ESPEJO
- CÓMODA
- MESA
- CORTINA
- COMÓDA
- ALFOMBRA
- BANQUILLO
- ESTANTE

4.

- DESPERTADOR
- ESTUFA
- GRIFO
- BOMBILLA
- NEVERA
- TELÉFONO
- TIMBRE
- PERCHA
- LUZ

5.

- CARTAS
- AJEDREZ
- TELENOVELA
- CABLE
- RADIO
- CUCIGRAMA
- DAMAS
- REVELE
- TELEVISOR
- LIBRO
- JUEGO

6.

- HIJO
- SUEGRA
- CUÑADA
- ABUELA
- NIETO
- TÍO
- MADRE
- HIJA
- TÍ
- CUÑADO
- SUEGRO
- ABUELO
- NIETA
- PADRE

7.

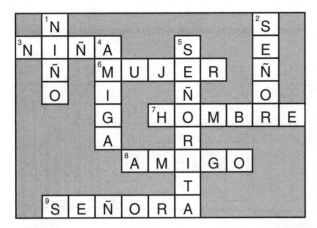

10.

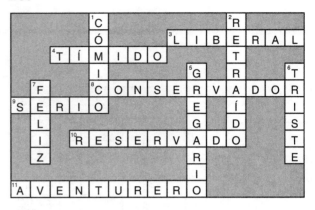

8.

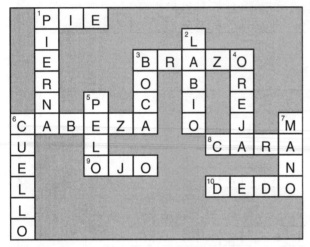

11.
once
veinte
cien
treinta
mil
setenta
catorce
siete
doscientos
noventa

12.
medianoche
mediodía
noche
día
las dos y media
las nueve
tarde
las ocho y cuarto
la una en punto
mañana

9.

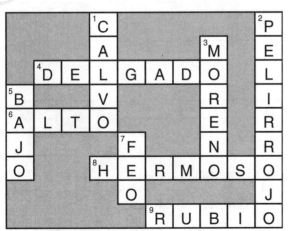

13.
Está nublado
Hace frío
Hace viento
Hace calor
Nieva
Llueve
Está despejado
Está húmedo
Truena
Hace fresco

14.
rojo
azul
verde
marrón
morado
blanco
negro
anaranjado
amarillo
rosado

15.
dulce
amargo
redondo
cuadrado
suave
duro
simpático
antipático
largo
corto

16.

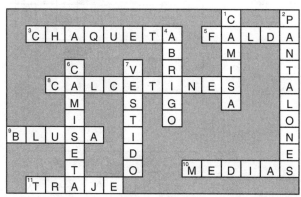

17.

18.

19.

20.

The key to the cryptogram follows. The following numbers correspond to the follow letters.

1 = A
2 = E
3 = I
4 = O
5 = U
6 = B
7 = C
8 = D
9 = F
10 = G
11 = H
12 = J
13 = L
14 = M
15 = N
16 = Ñ
17 = P
18 = Q
19 = R
20 = S
21 = T
22 = V
23 = X
24 = Y
25 = Z

21.
Hello! ¡Hola!
Good-bye! ¡Adiós!

22.
How are you? ¿Cómo estás?
Very well. Muy bien.

23.
My name is … Me llamo …
A pleasure. Encantado.

24.
Thank you very much. Muchas gracias.
You're welcome. De nada.

25.
Have a good trip! ¡Buen viaje!
Congratulations! ¡Felicitaciones!

26.

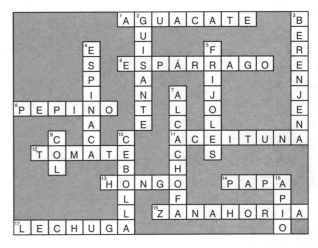

27.

28.

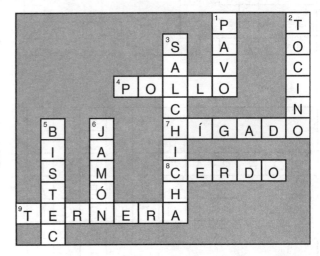

29.

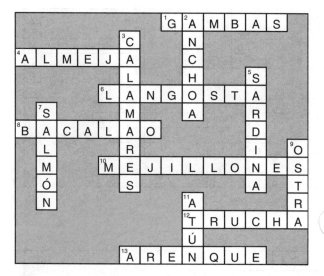

Across/Down answers:
- ¹GAMBAS
- ³C (CALAMARES)
- ²ANCHA
- ⁴ALMEJA
- ⁵S (SARDINA)
- ⁶LANGOSTA
- ⁷S (SALMÓN)
- ⁸BACALAO
- ⁹O (OSTRA)
- ¹⁰MEJILLONES
- ¹¹A (ATÚN)
- ¹²TRUCHA
- ¹³ARENQUE

30.

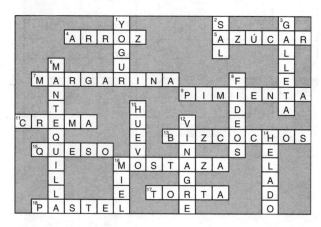

- ¹Y (YOGUR)
- ²S (SAL)
- ³G (GALLETA)
- ⁴ARROZ
- ⁵AZÚCAR
- ⁶M (MANTEQUILLA)
- ⁷MARGARINA
- ⁸F (FIDEOS)
- ⁹PIMIENTA
- ¹⁰H (HUEVIE?)
- ¹¹CREMA
- ¹²V (VINAGRE)
- ¹³BIZCOCHOS
- ¹⁴H (HELADO)
- ¹⁵QUESO
- ¹⁶MOSTAZA
- ¹⁷TORTA
- ¹⁸PASTEL

31.

- ¹T (TARDE)
- ²NUNCA
- ³T (TEMPRANO)
- ⁴SIEMPRE
- ⁵DESPACIO
- ⁶RÁPIDO

32.

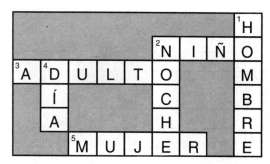

- ¹L (LEJOS)
- ²A (ADENTRAR)
- ³CERCA
- ⁴A (ARRIBA)
- ⁵A (AFUERER)
- ⁶ABAJO

33.

- ¹G (GORDADD)
- ²D (DELGADAJ)
- ³V (VIEJO)
- ⁴JOVEN
- ⁵B (B)
- ⁶FEO
- ⁷ALTO
- ⁸HERMOSO

34.

- ¹H (HOMBRE)
- ²NIÑO (NOCHCH)
- ³ADULTO
- ⁴DÍA
- ⁵MUJER

35.

```
      ¹R E C ²O R D A R
              D
      ³Q     I     ⁴V
       U     A     I
      ⁵P E R D E R     ⁶M
       R           V   O
      ⁷E N C O N T R A R
       R               R
          ⁸O L V I D A R
```

36.

```
¹R E F R E S ²C O     ³J
            E         U
            R         G
            ⁴V I N O
     ⁵L E ⁶C H E
         A   Z
         F   ⁷A G U A
         ⁸T É
```

37.

```
¹R E S E R V A ²C I Ó N
E             A
S             F
T     ³C A M A R E R A     ⁴C
A      U      T            A
U      E      E            M
R      N    ⁵P R O ⁶P I N A
A      T      Í    R       R
N      A      A    E       E
T                  C       R
E          ⁷S E R V I C I O
                   O
```

38.

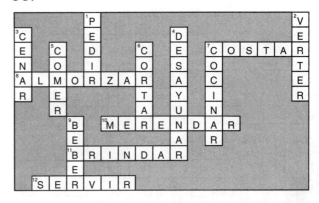

```
              ¹P                        ²V
   ³C     ⁵C   E     ⁴D         ⁷C O S T A R   E
   E N O  O   D   ⁶C E          O            R
   N   R  I   ⁸A L M O R Z A R  C            T
   A   E  T   R   T S A         I            E
   R      A       A A Y U       N            R
                    ⁹B ⁱ⁰M E R E N D A R
                    E        A
                   ¹¹B R I N D A R
                    E
                ¹²S E R V I R
```

39.

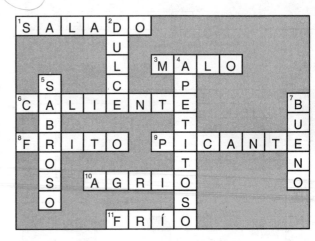

```
¹S A L A ²D O
         U
         L     ³M A L O
      ⁵S C     P
   ⁶C A L I E N T E         ⁷B
      B        T           U
   ⁸F R I T O  ⁹P I C A N T E N
      O        T           O
      S   ¹⁰A G R I O       N
      O        S           O
         ¹¹F R Í O
```

40.

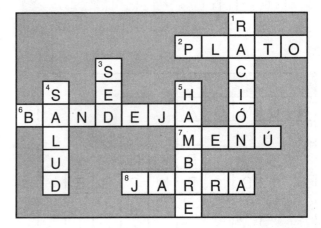

```
                    ¹R
              ²P L A T O
         ³S        C
    ⁴S   E    ⁵H   I
   ⁶B A N D E J A  Ó
    L U       ⁷M E N Ú
    U D  ⁸J A R R A
         ⁸    B
              E
```

41.

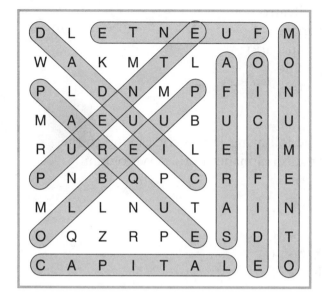

Words
afueras
capital
ciudad
edificio
fuente
monumento
parque
pueblo
puente

42.

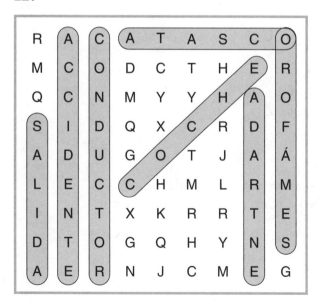

Words
accidente
atasco
coche
conductor
entrada
salida
semáforo

43.

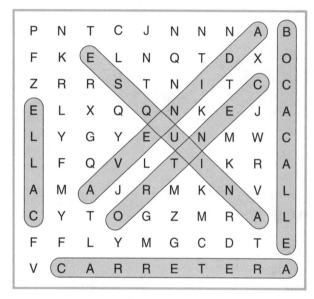

Words
avenida
bocacalle
calle
carretera
centro
esquina

44.

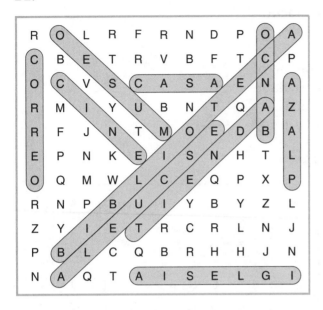

Words
anfiteatro
barrio
campanario
templo
torre

The following letters correspond to the Spanish alphabet in this cryptogram.

Z	=	A
Y	=	B
A	=	C
X	=	D
B	=	E
V	=	F
C	=	G
U	=	H
D	=	I
E	=	J
W	=	K
T	=	L
F	=	M
S	=	N
G	=	O
R	=	P
H	=	Q
Q	=	R
I	=	S
J	=	T
P	=	U
L	=	V
M	=	X
O	=	Y
N	=	Z

Words
banco
biblioteca
casa
cine
correo
escuela
iglesia
museo
plaza
tienda

45.

```
K  T  E  M  P  L  O  K  P  O
M  P  O  N  K  W  R  T  R  I
N  H  L  R  C  B  T  N  W  R
F  T  R  P  R  O  A  L  N  A
H  M  G  T  I  E  E  R  F  N
K  M  B  R  J  J  T  N  T  A
X  J  R  K  N  J  I  P  H  P
N  A  L  Q  V  G  F  L  K  M
B  J  P  T  X  K  N  Q  B  A
F  J  J  H  R  L  A  B  Q  C
```

46.
¡Buenos días! Good day!
No hay de qué. Don't mention it.

47.
¡Con permiso! Excuse me!
¡Perdón! Pardon me!

48.
¡Que pase buenas vacaciones! Have a good
    holiday!
¡Diviértase! Have a nice time!

49.
¡Claro que sí! Of course!
¡No lo puedo creer! I don't believe it!

50.
¡Salud! God bless you! (after a sneeze)
¡Pase usted! Come in!

51.

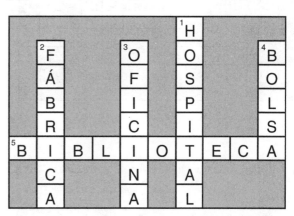

52.

53.

54.

55.

56.

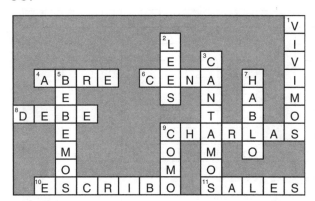

59.

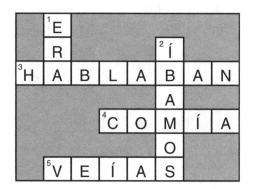

57.

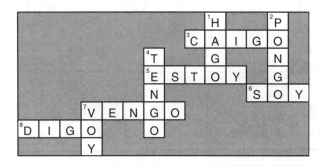

60.

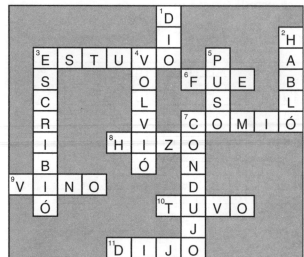

58.

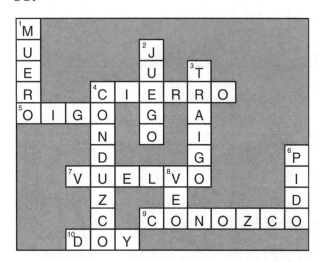

61.

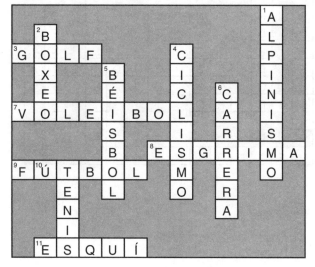

62.

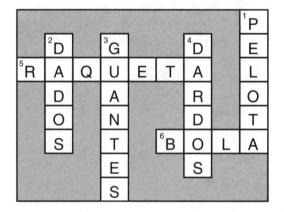

Crossword 62:
- 1 down: G
- 3 across: PISTA
- 2 down: ESTADIO
- 4 down: CAMPO
- 5 across: CANCHA
- 1 down: GIMNASIO
- 6 across: HIPÓDROMO

63.

Crossword 63:
- 1 down: PELOTA
- 2 down: DADOS
- 3 down: GUANTES
- 4 down: DARDOS
- 5 across: RAQUETA
- 6 across: BOLA

64.

Crossword 64:
- 1 down: CORRER
- 2 down: JUGAR
- 3 across: CAMINAR
- 3 down: CANTAR
- 4 down: BAILAR
- 5 across: LEER
- 6 across: PATINAR
- 7 down: NADAR
- 8 across: ACAMPAR
- 9 across: ESQUIAR

65.

Crossword 65:
- 1 down: NUMISMÁTICA
- 2 across: JUEGO
- 3 down: VIDEOJUEGO
- 4 across: BILLAR
- 5 down: NATACIÓN
- 6 across: AJEDREZ
- 7 down: CARA
- 8 across: FILATELIA
- 9 across: DAMAS

66.

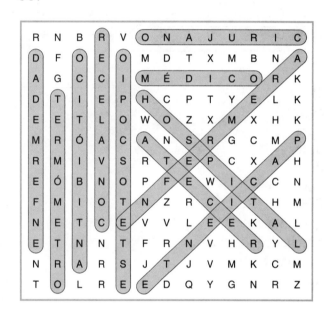

Words
antibiótico
cirujano
convalecer
enfermedad
enfermera
estetoscopio
hospital
médico
paciente
receta
termómetro

67.

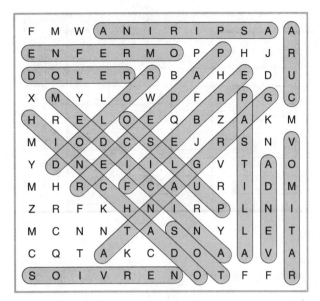

68.

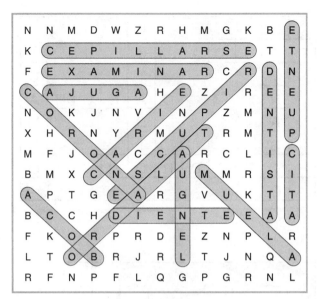

Words

aspirina
cura
doler
dolor
enfermo
fiebre
garganta
hinchado
medicina
nervios
padecer
pastilla
pulso
tos
venda
vomitar

Words

aguja
boca
carie
cepillarse
cita
corona
dentista
diente
examinar
escupir
lengua
muela
puente
taladro

69.

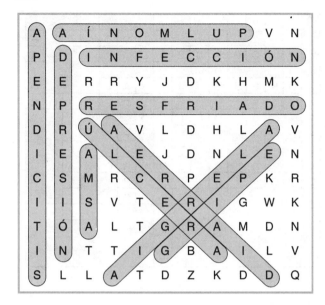

Words
alergia
apendicitis
asma
depresión
diarrea
gripe
infección
pulmonía
resfriado
úlcera

70.

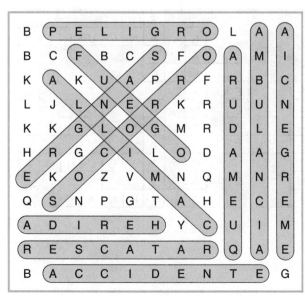

Words
accidente
ambulancia
camilla
emergencia
fuego
herida
peligro
quemadura
rescatar
sangre
socorro

71.

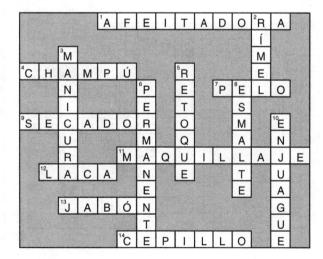

72.

73.

- 1 INDECISO
- 4 CELOSO
- 5 IRRITABLE
- 6 FELIZ
- 8 ENOJADO
- 9 TRISTE
- 10 IMPULSIVO
- 2 CARIÑOSO
- 3 SENSIBLE
- 7 INQUIETO

74.

- 1 INTELIGENTE
- 5 LISTO
- 6 SABIO
- 7 IDIOTA
- 2 ESTÚPIDO
- 3 GENIO
- 4 TONTO

75.

- 3 GENEROSO
- 9 EXTROVERTIDO
- 10 TÍMIDO
- 11 RESERVADO
- 1 TERCO
- 2 AGRESIVO
- 4 SIMPÁTICO
- 5 SINCERO
- 6 CÓMICO
- 7 ANTIPÁTICO
- 8 AMISTOSOS

76.

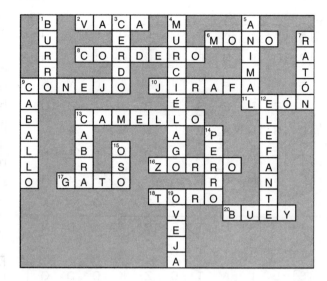

- 2 VACA
- 6 MONO
- 8 CORDERO
- 9 CONEJO
- 10 JIRAFA
- 11 LEÓN
- 13 CAMELLO
- 16 ZORRO
- 17 GATO
- 18 TORO
- 20 BUEY
- 1 BURRO
- 3 CERDO
- 4 MUCACA
- 5 AIMA
- 7 RATÓN
- 12 ELEFANTE
- 14 PERRO
- 15 OS
- 19 OVEJA
- CABALLO

77.

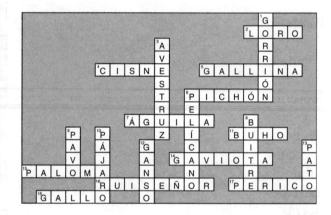

- 2 LORO
- 4 CISNE
- 5 GALLINA
- 6 PICHÓN
- 7 ÁGUILA
- 11 BUHO
- 14 GAVIOTA
- 15 PALOMA
- 16 RUISEÑOR
- 17 PERICO
- 18 GALLO
- 1 GORRIÓN
- 3 AVESTRUZ
- 8 BIO
- 9 PAVO
- 10 PÁJARO
- 12 GANANCA
- 13 PATO

78.

- 3 ANGUILA
- 4 PULPO
- 9 RANA
- 10 DELFÍN
- 11 TIBURÓN
- 12 BALLENA
- 1 SAPO
- 2 SALAMANDRA
- 5 FOCA
- 6 SARDINA
- 7 TORTIGA
- 8 REPTIL

79.

Across: CEREZO, HIGUERA, ÁLAMO, LIMONERO, DURAZNERO, PALMA, OLIVO, ÁRBOL

Down: ROBLE, PINO, MANZANO, ARCE, CIPRÉS, NARANJO, ABETO

80.

Across: ORQUÍDEA, GERANIO, FLOR, MARGARITA, PETUNIA, TULIPÁN, DALIA

Down: ROSA, VIOLETA, GLADIOLO, AZUCENA

81.

Across: CANTAR, TENER, BESAR, GRITAR, MIRAR

Down: ENTRAR, CONDUCIR, HABLAR, ESCRIBIR, VIAJAR

82.

Across: VENDER, PINTAR, DIBUJAR, ALMORZAR

Down: DESAYUNAR, COMPRAR, CENAR

83.

Across: LADRAR, RELINCHAR

Down: MAULLAR, RUGIR, AULLAR, BALAR

84.

GUATEMALTECO, ARGENTINO, MÉXICO, VENEZOLANO, PERUANO, URUGUAYO, SALVADOREÑO, PANAMEÑO, COSTARRICENSE, PARAGUAYO, HONDUREÑO, BOLIVIANO, CUBANO, CHILENO, NICARAGÜENSE, COLOMBIANO, DOMINICANO, PUERTORRIQUEÑO, ESPAÑOL, NORTEAMERICANO

85.

88.

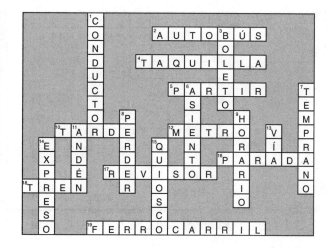

86.

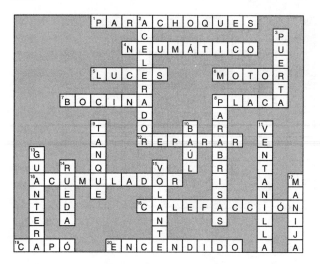

89.

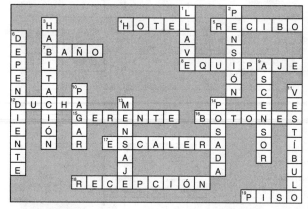

87.

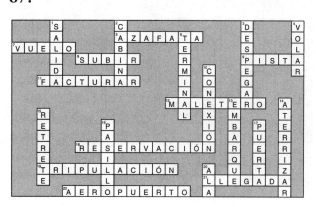

90.

91.

92.

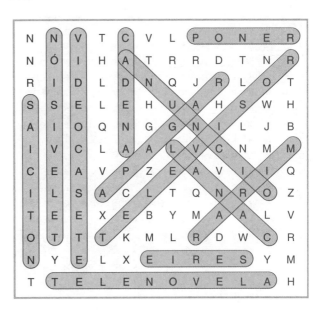

Words
archivo
compatible
computadora
cursor
datos
disco
escáner
función
icono
impresora
instalar
interruptor
memoria
monitor
módem
procesador
programa
ratón
teclado

Words
anuncio
apagar
cadena
canal
mirar
noticias
poner
serie
telenovela
televisión
televisor
videocasete

93.

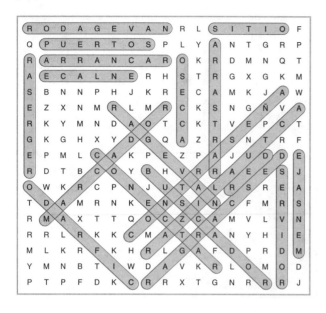

94.

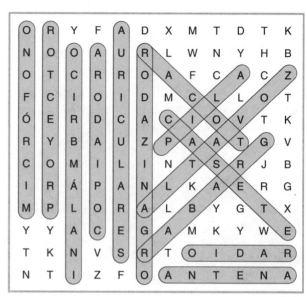

Words

acceso
actualizar
arrancar
arrastrar
buscador
cifrado
conectar
contraseña
descargar
enlace
marcador
mensaje
navegador
navegar
puertos
red
regresar
servidor
sitio

Words

altavoz
antena
auriculares
casete
copiadora
grabar
inalámbrico
micrófono
organizador
pila
proyector
radio
tocar

95.

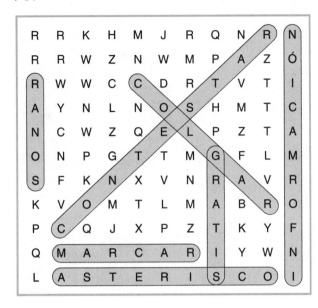

Words
asterisco
colgar
contestar
gratis
información
marcar
sonar

The corresponding alphabetic letters for this cryptogram are the following.

Z	=	A
Y	=	B
A	=	C
X	=	D
B	=	E
V	=	F
C	=	G
U	=	H
D	=	I
E	=	J
W	=	K
T	=	L
F	=	M
S	=	N
G	=	O
R	=	P
H	=	Q
Q	=	R
I	=	S
J	=	T
P	=	U
L	=	V
M	=	X
O	=	Y
N	=	Z

96.
Cervantes
García Márquez

97.
Picasso
Kahlo

98.
Estefan
Santana

99.
La Bamba
Cruz

100.
Banderas
Rodríguez

Word Finder

The following words and expressions are the ones needed to solve the puzzles. They are listed here for your convenience. The number in parentheses after the Spanish word indicates the puzzle where the word or phrase may be found.

A

a pleasure	encantado (23)
above	arriba (32)
access	acceso (93)
accident	accidente (42, 70)
ache	dolor (67)
actor	actor (51)
adult	adulto (34)
adventurous	aventurero (10)
affectionate	cariñoso (73)
afternoon	tarde (12)
afuera	outside (32)
aggressive	agresivo (75)
airport	aeropuerto (87)
aisle	pasillo (87)
alarm clock	despertador (4)
allergy	alergia (69)
always	siempre (31)
ambulance	ambulancia (70)
amphitheater	anfiteatro (45)
anchovy	anchoa (29)
angry	enojado (73)
animal	animal (76)
answer (to)	contestar (95)
antenna	antena (94)
antibiotic	antibiótico (66)
anxious	inquieto (73)
appendicitis	apendicitis (69)
appetizing	apetitoso (39)
apple	manzana (27)
apple tree	manzano (79)
appointment	cita (68)
apricot	albaricoque (27)

architect	arquitecto (51)
Argentine	argentino (84)
arm	brazo (8)
armchair	sillón (3)
arrival	llegada (87)
artichoke	alcachofa (26)
asparagus	espárrago (26)
aspirin	aspirina (67)
asthma	asma (69)
aunt	tía (6)
avenue	avenida (43)
avocado	aguacate (26)

B

bacon	tocino (28)
bad	malo (39)
bakery	panadería (85)
bald	calvo (9)
banana	banana (27)
bandage	venda (67)
bank	banco (44)
banker	banquero (51)
barber	barbero (71)
barber shop	barbería (71)
bark (to)	ladrar (83)
baseball	béisbol (61)
baseball	pelota (63)
basement	sótano (1)
bat	murciélago (76)
bathroom	baño (89)
battery	acumulador (86)
battery	pila (94)
beach	playa (90)
beans	frijoles (26)
bear	oso (76)
beautician	peluquero (71)
beautiful	hermoso (9, 33)
beauty shop	peluquería (71)
bed	cama (3)
bedroom	alcoba (1)
beer	cerveza (36)

bell tower	campanario (45)	**C**	
bellboy	botones (89)	cabbage	col (26)
below	abajo (32)	cabin	cabina (87)
belt	cinturón (17)	cable	cable (5)
bicycle racing	ciclismo (61)	cafeteria	cafetería (37)
bill	cuenta (37)	cake	torta (30)
billiards	billar (65)	calendar	calendario (53)
bird	pájaro (77)	camel	camello (76)
biscuit	bizcocho (30)	camp (to)	acampar (64)
bitter	amargo (15)	campground	campamento (90)
black	negro (14)	capital	capital (41)
bleat (to)	balar (83)	car	coche (42)
blond	rubio (9)	car window	ventanilla (86)
blood	sangre (70)	cards	cartas (5)
blouse	blusa (16)	career	carrera (55)
blue	azul (14)	carpenter	carpintero (52)
board (to)	subir (87)	carrot	zanahoria (26)
boarding	embarque (87)	cassette	casete (94)
boardinghouse	pensión (89)	cat	gato (76)
Bolivian	bolivano (84)	cavity	carie (68)
book	libro (5)	ceiling	techo (1)
bookcase	estante (3)	celery	apio (26)
bookmark	marcador (93)	chain	cadena (18)
bookstore	librería (85)	chair	silla (53)
boot (to)	arrancar (93)	channel	canal (92)
boots	botas (19)	check	cuenta (37)
boss	jefe (55)	check (to)	facturar (87)
bottle	botella (2)	checkers	damas (5, 65)
bowling ball	bola (63)	Cheers!	¡Salud! (40)
boxing	boxeo (61)	cheese	queso (30)
bracelet	pulsera (18)	cherry	cereza (27)
bridge	puente (41, 68)	cherry tree	cerezo (79)
brooch	broche (18)	chess	ajedrez (5, 65)
brother-in-law	cuñado (6)	chest of drawers	cómoda (3)
brown	marrón (14)	chicken	pollo (28)
brunette	moreno (9)	child	niño (34)
brush	cepillo (72)	child (female)	niña (7)
brush oneself (to)	cepillarse (68, 71)	child (male)	niño (7)
building	edificio (41)	Chilean	chileno (84)
bull	toro (76)	church	iglesia (44)
bumper	parachoques (86)	city	ciudad (41)
burn	quemadura (70)	clam	almeja (29)
bus	autobús (88)	clean (to)	limpiar (71)
bus driver	conductor (88)	closet	armario (1)
butcher	carnicero (52)	coat	abrigo (16)
butcher shop	carnicería (85)	codfish	bacalao (29)
butter	mantequilla (30)	coffee	café (36)
buy (to)	comprar (82)	coffeepot	cafetera (2)

coin collecting	numismática (65)	day	día (12, 34)
cold	frío (39)	dentist	dentista (52, 68)
cold	resfriado (69)	departure	salida (87)
Colombian	colombiano (84)	depression	depresión (69)
comb oneself (to)	peinarse (71)	desk	escritorio (53)
Come in!	¡Pase usted! (50)	dial (to)	marcar (95)
commerce	comercio (55)	diarrhea	diarrea (69)
commercial	anuncio (92)	dice	dados (63)
company	compañía (55)	die (to)	morir (35)
compatible	compatible (91)	dining room	comedor (1)
computer	computadora (53, 91)	dish	plato (40)
Congratulations!	¡Felicitaciones!(25)	disk	disco (91)
connect (to)	conectar (93)	doctor	médico (51, 66)
connection	conexión (87)	dog	perro (76)
conservative	conservador (10)	dolphin	delfín (78)
convalesce	convalecer (66)	Dominican	dominicano (84)
cook	cocinero (51)	donkey	burro (76)
cook (to)	cocinar (38)	Don't mention it.	No hay de qué. (46)
cookie	galleta (30)		
copier	copiadora (94)	door	puerta (1, 86)
corner	esquina (43)	doorbell	timbre (4)
cost (to)	costar (38)	dove	paloma (77)
Costa Rican	costarricense (84)	download (to)	descargar (93)
cough	tos (67)	downtown	centro (43)
course	plato (40)	drag (to)	arrastrar (93)
cow	vaca (76)	drawer	cajón (3)
cream	crema (30)	dress	vestido (16)
crew	tripulación (87)	dresser	tocador (3)
crossword puzzle	crucigrama (5)	drill	taladro (68)
crown	corona (68)	drink (to)	beber (38)
cruise	crucero (90)	drive (to)	conducir (81)
Cuban	cubano (84)	driver	conductor (42)
cucumber	pepino (26)	dry (to)	secar (71)
cure	cura (67)	duck	pato (77)
cursor	cursor (91)		
curtain	cortina (3)	E	
cut (to)	cortar (38, 71)	eagle	águila (77)
cypress	ciprés (79)	ear	oreja (8)
		early	temprano (31, 88)
D		earn (to)	ganar (55)
dahlia	dalia (80)	earring	arete (18)
dairy	lechería (85)	eat (to)	comer (38)
daisy	margarita (80)	Ecuadorian	ecuatoriano (84)
dance (to)	bailar (64)	eel	anguila (78)
danger	peligro (70)	egg	huevo (30)
darts	dardos (63)	eggplant	berenjena (26)
data	datos (91)	eight fifteen	las ocho y cuarto (12)
daughter	hija (6)		

electrician	electricista (52)
elephant	elefante (76)
elevator	ascensor (89)
eleven	once (11)
emergency	emergencia (70)
employee	empleado (55)
encrypted	cifrado (93)
engine	motor (86)
enter (to)	entrar (81)
entrance	entrada (42)
examine (to)	examinar (68)
Excuse me!	¡Con permiso! (47)
exit	salida (42)
express	expreso (88)
eye	ojo (8)

F

face	cara (8)
factory	fábrica (54)
factory worker	obrero (52)
far away	lejos (32)
fast	rápido (31)
fat	gordo (33)
father	padre (6)
father-in-law	suegro (6)
faucet	grifo (4)
fencing	esgrima (61)
fever	fiebre (67)
fig	higo (27)
fig tree	higuera (79)
file	archivo (53, 91)
find (to)	encontrar (35)
finger	dedo (8)
fir tree	abeto (79)
fire	fuego (70)
fire (to)	echar (55)
firefighter	bombero (51)
fish (in water)	pez (78)
fish (to)	pescar (90)
fish store	pescadería (85)
flight	vuelo (87)
flight attendant	azafata (87)
floor	piso (89)
floor	suelo (1)
flower	flor (80)
flu	gripe (69)
fly (to)	volar (87)
fool	tonto (74)

foot	pie (8)
forget (to)	olvidar (35)
fork	tenedor (2)
fountain	fuente (41)
fourteen	catorce (11)
fox	zorro (76)
fried	frito (39)
friend (female)	amiga (7)
friend (male)	amigo (7)
friendly	amistoso (75)
frog	rana (78)
fruit store	frutería (85)
function	función (91)
funny	cómico (10, 75)

G

game	juego (5, 65)
gas pedal	acelerador (86)
gas tank	tanque (86)
gate	puerta (87)
generous	generoso (75)
genius	genio (74)
geranium	geranio (80)
get dressed (to)	vestirse (20)
giraffe	jirafa (76)
gladiolus	gladiolo (80)
glass	vaso (2)
glove	guante (17)
glove compartment	guantera (86)
gloves (boxing, baseball)	guantes (63)
go back (to)	regresar (93)
goat	cabra (76)
God bless you!	¡Salud! (50)
golf	golf (61)
good	bueno (39)
Good day!	¡Buenos días! (46)
Good-bye!	Adiós (21)
goose	ganso (77)
granddaughter	nieta (6)
grandfather	abuelo (6)
grandmother	abuela (6)
grandson	nieto (6)
grapefruit	toronja (27)
green	verde (14)
gregarious	gregario (10)
Guatemalan	guatemalteco (84)

H	
hair	pelo (8, 72)
hair dryer	secador (72)
hair spray	laca (72)
hairdresser	peluquero (51, 71)
ham	jamón (28)
hand	mano (8)
handkerchief	pañuelo (17)
handle	manija (86)
hang up (to)	colgar (95)
hanger	percha (4)
happy	feliz (10, 73)
hard	duro (15)
hat	sombrero (17)
hate (to)	odiar (35)
have (to)	tener (81)
Have a good holiday!	¡Que pase buenas vacaciones! (48)
Have a good trip!	¡Buen viaje! (25)
Have a nice time!	¡Diviértase! (48)
have a snack (to)	merendar (38)
have breakfast (to)	desayunar (38, 82)
have dinner (to)	cenar (38, 82)
have lunch (to)	almorzar (38, 82)
he ate	comió (60)
he came	vino (60)
he did	hizo (60)
he drove	condujo (60)
he gave	dio (60)
he had	tuvo (60)
he put	puso (60)
he returned (*volver*)	volvió (60)
he said	dijo (60)
he spoke	habló (60)
he was (*estar*)	estuvo (60)
he went	fue (60)
he wrote	escribió (60)
head	cabeza (8)
headphones	auriculares (94)
heating	calefacción (86)
heel	tacón (19)
Hello!	¡Hola! (21)
Help!	¡Socorro! (70)
hen	gallina (77)
herring	arenque (29)
highway	carretera (43)
hire (to)	contratar (55)
Honduran	hondureño (84)

honey	miel (30)
hood	capó (86)
horn	bocina (86)
horse	caballo (76)
hospital	hospital (54, 66)
hot (warm)	caliente (39)
hotel clerk	dependiente (89)
hotel	hotel (89)
house	casa (1, 44)
How are you?	¿Qué tal? (22)
hundred	cien (11)
hunger	hambre (40)
hurt (to)	doler (67)
I	
I am (*estar*)	estoy (57)
I am (*ser*)	soy (57)
I bring	traigo (58)
I close	cierro (58)
I come	vengo (57)
I die	muero (58)
I do	hago (57)
I don't believe it!	¡No lo puedo creer! (49)
I drive (*conducir*)	conduzco (58)
I eat	como (56)
I fall	caigo (57)
I give	doy (58)
I go	voy (57)
I have	tengo (57)
I hear	oigo (58)
I know (*conocer*)	conozco (58)
I order	pido (58)
I play (*jugar*)	juego (58)
I put	pongo (57)
I return (*volver*)	vuelvo (58)
I say	digo (57)
I see	veo (58)
I speak	hablo (56)
I was	era (59)
I write	escribo (56)
ice cream	helado (30)
ice cream parlor	heladería (85)
icon	ícono (91)
idiot	idiota (74)
ignition	encendido (86)
illness	enfermedad (66)
impulsive	impulsivo (73)

indecisive	indeciso (73)
infection	infección (69)
information	información (95)
injury	herida (70)
inn	posada (89)
inside	adentro (32)
install (to)	instalar (91)
intelligent	inteligente (74)
intersection	bocacalle (43)
irritable	irritable (73)
It's humid.	Está húmedo. (13)
It's clear.	Está despejado. (13)
It's cloudy.	Está nublado. (13)
It's cold.	Hace frío. (13)
It's cool.	Hace fresco. (13)
It's hot.	Hace calor. (13)
It's raining.	Llueve. (13)
It's snowing.	Nieva. (13)
It's thundering.	Truena. (13)
It's windy.	Hace viento. (13)

J

jacket	chaqueta (16)
jealous	celoso (73)
journalist	periodista (52)
juice	jugo (36)

K

keyboard	teclado (91)
key	llave (89)
kiss (to)	besar (81)
kitchen	cocina (1)
knife	cuchillo (2)

L

lake	lago (90)
lamb	cordero (76)
lamp	lámpara (3)
land (to)	aterrizar (87)
late	tarde (31, 88)
lawyer	abogado (51)
leave (to)	partir (88)
leg	pierna (8)
lemon	limón (27)
lemon tree	limonero (79)
lettuce	lechuga (26)
liberal	liberal (10)
library	biblioteca (44, 54)

license plate	placa (86)
light	luz (4)
lightbulb	bombilla (4)
lights	luces (86)
lily	acuzena (80)
link	enlace (93)
lion	león (76)
lip	labio (8)
live (to)	vivir (35)
liver	hígado (28)
living room	sala (1)
lobby	vestíbulo (89)
lobster	langosta (29)
long	largo (15)
look at (to)	mirar (81)
lose (to)	perder (35)
love (to)	querer (35)
luggage	equipaje (89)

M

makeup	maquillaje (72)
man	hombre (7, 34)
manager	gerente (55, 89)
manicure	manicura (72)
maple tree	arce (79)
margarine	margarina (30)
mascara	rimel (72)
mechanic	mecánico (51)
medicine	medicina (67)
melon	melón (27)
memory	memoria (91)
menu	menú (40)
meow (to)	maullar (83)
message	mensaje (89, 93)
Mexican	mexicano (84)
microphone	micrófono (94)
midnight	medianoche (12)
milk	leche (36)
mirror	espejo (3)
miss	señorita (7)
miss (to)	perder (88)
mister	señor (7)
modem	módem (91)
molar	muela (68)
monitor	monitor (91)
monkey	mono (76)
monument	monumento (41)
morning	mañana (12)

mother	madre (6)		olive tree	olivo (79)
mother-in-law	suegra (6)		one o'clock sharp	la una en punto (12)
motor	motor (86)			
mountain climbing	alpinismo (61)		onion	cebolla (26)
mountains	montañas (90)		orange	anaranjado (14)
mouse	ratón (76, 91)		orange	naranja (27)
mouth	boca (8, 68)		orange tree	naranjo (79)
movie theater	cine (44)		orchid	orquídea (80)
Mrs.	Señora (7)		order (to)	pedir (38)
museum	museo (44)		organizer	organizador (94)
mushroom	hongo (26)		ostrich	avestruz (77)
musician	músico (51)		outgoing	extrovertido (75)
mussels	mejillones (29)		owl	buho (77)
mustard	mostaza (30)		ox	buey (76)
My name is …	Me llamo … (23)		oyster	ostra (29)

N

nail polish	esmalte (72)
napkin	servilleta (2)
nearby	cerca (32)
neck	cuello (8)
necklace	collar (18)
needle	aguja (68)
neigh (to)	relinchar (83)
neighborhood	barrio (45)
nerves	nervios (67)
net	red (93)
network	cadena (92)
never	nunca (31)
news	noticias (92)
newsstand	quiosco (88)
Nicaraguan	nicaragüense (84)
nice	simpático (15, 75)
night	noche (12, 34)
nightingale	ruiseñor (77)
nine o'clock	las nueve (12)
ninety	noventa (11)
noodles	fideos (30)
noon	mediodía (12)
nurse	enfermera (66)

O

oak tree	roble (79)
octopus	pulpo (78)
Of course!	¡Claro que sí! (49)
office	oficina (54)
old	viejo (33)
olive	aceituna (26)

P

paint (to)	pintar (82)
palm tree	palma (79)
Panamanian	panameño (84)
pantry	despensa (1)
pants	pantalones (16)
Paraguayan	paraguayo (84)
parakeet	perico (77)
Pardon me!	¡Perdón! (47)
park	parque (41)
parrot	loro (77)
password	contraseña (93)
pastry shop	pastelería (85)
patient	paciente (66)
pay (to)	pagar (89)
pea	guisante (26)
peach	melocotón (27)
peach tree	duraznero (79)
pelican	pelícano (77)
pen	bolígrafo (53)
pencil	lápiz (53)
pepper	pimienta (30)
pepper shaker	pimentero (2)
permanent	permanente (72)
Peruvian	peruano (84)
petunia	petunia (80)
pharmacy	farmacia (85)
photocopier	fotocopiadora (53)
pie	pastel (30)
piece of furniture	mueble (3)
pig	cerdo (76)
pigeon	pichón (77)

sardine	sardina (29, 78)	soap	jabón (72)
saucer	platillo (2)	soap opera	telenovela (5, 92)
sausage	salchicha (28)	soccer	fútbol (61)
scanner	escáner (91)	socks	calcetines (16)
scarf	bufanda (17)	soft	suave (15)
schedule	horario (88)	soft drink	refresco (36)
school	escuela (44)	sole	suela (19)
scissors	tijeras (53)	son	hijo (6)
sea	mar (90)	sour	agrio (39)
seagull	gaviota (77)	Spaniard	español (84)
seal	foca (78)	sparrow	gorrión (77)
search engine	buscador (93)	speak (to)	hablar (81)
seat	asiento (88)	speaker	altavoz (94)
sell (to)	vender (82)	spicy	picante (39)
sensitive	sensible (73)	spinach	espinaca (26)
series	serie (92)	spit	escupir (68)
serious	serio (10)	spoon	cuchara (2)
serve (to)	servir (38)	square	cuadrado (15)
server	servidor (93)	squids	calamares (29)
service	servicio (37)	stairway	escalera (89)
seven	siete (11)	stamp collecting	filatelia (65)
seventy	setenta (11)	star	asterisco (95)
shampoo	champú (72)	steak	bistec (28)
shark	tiburón (78)	steering wheel	volante (86)
sheep	oveja (76)	stethoscope	estetoscopio (66)
ship	barco (90)	stock exchange	bolsa (54)
shirt	camisa (16)	stockings	medias (16)
shoelaces	cordones (19)	stool	banquillo (3)
shoes	zapatos (19)	stop	parada (88)
short	bajo (9, 33)	store	tienda (44)
short	corto (15)	stove	estufa (4)
shout (to)	gritar (81)	strawberry	fresa (27)
shower	ducha (89)	street	calle (43)
shrimp	gambas (29)	stretcher	camilla (70)
shy	tímido (10, 75)	stubborn	terco (75)
sick	enfermo (67)	study	despacho (1)
sincere	sincero (75)	stupid	estúpido (74)
sing (to)	cantar (64, 81)	suburbs	afueras (41)
sister-in-law	cuñada (6)	subway	metro (88)
site	sitio (93)	suffer (to)	sufrir (67)
skate (to)	patinar (64)	sugar	azúcar (30)
sketch (to)	dibujar (82)	suit	traje (16)
ski	esquí (61)	surf (to)	navegar (93)
ski (to)	esquiar (64)	surgeon	cirujuano (66)
skirt	falda (16)	swan	cisne (77)
slender	delgado (9, 33)	sweet	dulce (15, 39)
slow	despacio (31)	swim (to)	nadar (64, 90)
smart	listo (74)	swimming	natación (65)

switch off (to)	apagar (92)	track	vía (88)
switch on (to)	poner (92)	traffic jam	atasco (42)
swollen	hinchado (67)	traffic light	semáforo (42)
		train	tren (88)
T		travel (to)	viajar (81)
table	mesa (2, 3)	tray	bandeja (40)
tablecloth	mantel (2)	tree	árbol (79)
tablet	pastilla (67)	trim (to)	recortar (71)
take off	quitarse (20)	trip	viaje (90)
take off (to)	despegar (87)	trout	trucha (29)
tall	alto (9, 33)	trunk	baúl (86)
tasty	sabroso (39)	try on (to)	probar (20)
tea	té (36)	t-shirt	camiseta (16)
teacher	maestro (51)	tulip	tulipán (80)
teapot	tetera (2)	tuna	atún (29)
telephone	teléfono (4, 53)	turkey	pavo (28, 77)
television	televisión (5, 92)	turtle	tortuga (78)
television set	televisor (92)	twenty	veinte (11)
temple	templo (45)	two hundred	doscientos (11)
tennis	tenis (61)	two thirty	las dos y media
tennis racket	raqueta (63)		(12)
terminal	terminal (87)		
Thank you very		**U**	
much.	Muchas gracias. (24)	ugly	feo (9, 33)
thermometer	termómetro (66)	ulcer	úlcera (69)
they were talking	hablaban (59)	uncle	tío (6)
thirst	sed (40)	undress oneself (to)	desnudarse (20)
thirty	treinta (11)	unpleasant	antipático (15, 75)
thousand	mil (11)	upgrade (to)	actualizar (93)
throat	garganta (67)	Uruguayan	uruguayo (84)
throw up (to)	vomitar (67)		
ticket	boleto (88)	**V**	
ticket checker	revisor (88)	vacations	vacaciones (90)
ticket counter	taquilla (88)	veal	ternera (28)
tie	corbata (17)	Venezuelan	venezolano (84)
tip	propina (37)	very well	muy bien (22)
tire	neumático (86)	veterinarian	veterinario (52)
toad	sapo (78)	video game	videojuego (65)
toast (to)	brindar (38)	videocassette	videocasete (92)
toilet	retrete (87)	vinegar	vinagre (30)
toll-free	gratis (95)	violet	violeta (80)
tomato	tomate (26)	volleyball	voleibol (61)
tongue	lengua (68)	vulture	buitre (77)
tooth	diente (68)		
touch up	retoque (72)	**W**	
tower	torre (45)	waiter	camarero (37)
town	pueblo (41)	waitress	camarera (37)
town square	plaza (44)	walk (to)	caminar (64)

wall	pared (1)	withdrawn	retraído (10)
wash (to)	lavar (71)	woman	mujer (7, 34)
wastebasket	papelero (53)	work	trabajo (55)
watch	reloj (18)	work associate	colega (55)
watch (to)	mirar (92)	write (to)	escribir (81)
water	agua (36)	writing desk	escritorio (3)
watermelon	sandía (27)		
we are drinking	bebemos (56)	**Y**	
we live	vivimos (56)	yellow	amarillo (14)
we were going	íbamos (59)	yogurt	yogur (30)
wear (to)	llevar (20)	you *(tú)* are reading	lees (56)
web	red (5)	you *(tú)* chat	charlas (56)
web browser	navegador (93)	you *(tú)* leave	sales (56)
whale	ballena (78)	you *(tú)* were seeing	veías (59)
wheel	rueda (86)	you *(usted)* are	
white	blanco (14)	dining	cena (56)
window	ventana (1)	you *(usted)* open	abre (56)
windshield	parabrisas (86)	you *(usted)*	
wine	vino (36)	ought/should	debe (56)
wineglass	copa (2)	you *(usted)* were	
wing	ala (87)	eating	comía (59)
wireless	inalámbrico (94)	young	joven (33)
wise	sabio (74)	You're welcome.	De nada. (24)

Break the Foreign Language Barrier with Barron's Language Series!

VERB SERIES

Over 300 of the most frequently used verbs in six foreign languages are presented in handy reference guides. Each guide displays fully conjugated verbs in all their forms, arranged alphabetically for quick and easy location. The idioms and expressions related to each verb are listed at the bottom of each page. A helpful index listing approximately 1000 additional verbs is included in each book. Here is wonderful review material for students, travelers, and business people.

Each book: $5.95–$7.95,
Can.$7.95–$11.50
French Verbs
German Verbs
Italian Verbs
Spanish Verbs

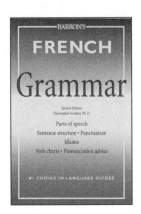

GRAMMAR SERIES

A comprehensive study of the elements of grammar and usage in six prominent languages makes these handy reference guides ideal for anyone just beginning a language study and those who wish to review what they've already learned. Parts of speech, sentence structure, lists of synonyms and antonyms, idiomatic phrases, days, dates, numbers, and much more are all reviewed. Also featured are guides to word pronunciation and sentence punctuation in each of the languages.

French Grammar, $5.95, Can.$8.50
German Grammar, $7.95, Can.$11.50
Italian Grammar, $6.95, Can.$8.95
Japanese Grammar, $6.95, Can.$8.95
Russian Grammar, $6.95, Can.$8.95
Spanish Grammar, $5.95, Can.$8.50

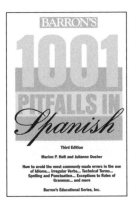

1001 PITFALLS SERIES

An all-inclusive series that eliminates frustration by effectively helping the beginning or advanced student through the most troublesome aspects of learning a foreign language. Overcome the difficult details of grammar, usage and style in three important European languages, with consistent use of these guides. Ideal for both individual and classroom use as a supplement to regular textbooks.

1001 Pitfalls in French,
3rd, $13.95, Can.$19.95

1001 Pitfalls in German,
3rd, $12.95, Can.$18.95

1001 Pitfalls in Spanish,
3rd, $10.95, Can.$14.50

Books may be purchased at your bookstore, or by mail from Barron's. Enclose check or money order for the total amount plus sales tax where applicable and 18% for postage and handling charge (minimum charge $5.95, Canada $4.00). New York, New Jersey, Michigan, and California residents add sales tax. Prices subject to change without notice.
ISBN PREFIX 0-8120 Can$ = Price in Canadian Dollars

Barron's Educational Series, Inc.
250 Wireless Blvd., Hauppauge, NY 11788
In Canada: Georgetown Book Warehouse
34 Armstrong Ave., Georgetown, Ontario L7G 4R9

R 10/05